# A Canoeing and Kayaking Guide to the Streams of Florida

# A Canoeing and Kayaking Guide to the Streams of Florida

## Volume II: Central and South Peninsula

Lou Glaros and
Doug Sphar

**Menasha Ridge Press**
Birmingham, Alabama

Printed in the United States of America
Published by Menasha Ridge Press
Distributed by The Globe Pequot Press
First edition, eighth printing, 2002


**Library of Congress Cataloging-in-Publication Data**
Carter, Elizabeth F., 1939–
A canoeing and kayaking guide to the streams of Florida

Vol. 2 has imprint: Birmingham, Ala. : Menasha Ridge Press.
Bibliography: v. 2, p.131
Includes Indexes.
Contents: v. 1. The North Central Panhandle and Peninsula—v. 2.
Central and south peninsula/Lou Glaros and Doug Sphar.
1. Canoes and canoeing—Florida—Guide-books.
2. Rivers—Description and travel—1981—Guide-books.   I. Pearce,
John L., 1936–.   II. Glaros, Lou.   III. Title.
GV776.F7C37 1985    917.59              85-11596
ISBN 0-89732-033-6 (pbk. : v. 1)
ISBN 0-89732-067-0 (pbk. : v. 2)

Cover photo by Carol Casey.
Photos on pages 47, 53, 55 and 63 by R. Edward DeBerry;
photos on pages 10, 13, 42, 51, 67, 72, 86 and 105 by Lou
Glaros; all other photos in book by Doug Sphar.

Menasha Ridge Press
P.O. Box 43673
Birmingham, AL 35243
www.menasharidge.com

*This book is dedicated to the memory of Kiki Glaros, who had absolutely nothing to do with canoes or paddling, but who was such a wonderful person that she deserves to have at least one book dedicated to her.*

*This dedication also recognizes two wonderful parents: Libby and Bud Sphar.*

# Contents

# Acknowledgments

As we put the finishing touches on this book, we look back over the past year and recognize a number of fine people who richly deserve our gratitude for their help. First and foremost, our deepest appreciation goes to Carol Glaros who not only aided us by editing and helping with the word processing, but also inspired and guided us when we really needed it. She also happens to be a wonderful paddling partner. Next, special thanks are extended to Mike Galt for convincing us to take on this project in the first place, and to Debbie and Ed DeBerry, great friends who were very helpful. We would also like to thank Mike and Tracy Davenport, Lou Danos, Jason Elliott, Melissa Glaros, Bill Brown, and Karl and Betty Eichhorn for their efforts in researching and paddling some of the streams, setting up long shuttles, or gathering information.

# Introduction

The state of Florida is an ecologically diverse area with an almost infinite number of opportunities for the outdoor enthusiast. Anglers can choose between saltwater fishing, along either the Atlantic or Gulf coasts, and freshwater fishing on the myriad of lakes and inland waterways. An established system of trails stretching across the state provides the day hiker and backpacker with routes that traverse some of the most unique terrain in the country. Quaint country roads are ideal for cyclists, while coastal estuaries and interior marshlands are a haven for birders of all skill levels.

Florida's water resources are among its most significant assets; the enthusiastic canoeist or kayaker has an abundance of rivers, creeks, estuaries, and lakes to explore. One of the most unique features of the waterways of Florida is diversity in character. Any given stream is likely to pass through numerous scenic areas as upland pine forests give way to dense oak hammocks, mixed hardwood swamps, and, eventually, coastal marshes. On some rivers the paddler will first cross sluggish flatwater and quiet pools, and then be confronted by a series of small rapids formed by limestone embedded in the river bottom. On many Florida streams, portages or carry-overs are often required, while on others the main channel separates into an interesting maze of braided pathways. Adding to the beauty is the wildlife. Paddling is an ideal way to visit the wilderness areas populated by alligators, deer, and wild turkey—where river otters streak through the water, often stopping to coax each other into a playful game.

It is the purpose of this book to provide the interested canoeist or kayaker with a convenient and up-to-date reference guide for the rivers and streams of central and south Florida. Years ago, under the guise of the Florida Canoe Trail System, the state published a guidebook that listed 35 waterways and their associated access points. Unfortunately, due to funding constraints, the booklet was not kept up-to-date, and all that is currently available is a photocopied brochure containing limited information.

In 1985, Elizabeth Carter and John Pearce wrote a guidebook entitled *A Canoeing and Kayaking Guide to the Streams of Florida, Volume I: North Central Peninsula and Panhandle*

1

(Menasha Ridge Press). That excellent work described over 30 rivers and streams in north Florida and is considered by many paddlers to be the definitive reference book for trip planning in that region of the state.

That guide was the precursor to this volume, which extends the coverage into the central and south peninsula. Twenty-six waterways have been included in this book. They range from the broad, open rivers that flow into tidal marshes to the tight creeks that snake through dense swamp and challenge the paddler's maneuvering skills.

In writing this book, our intent was to cover a selection of rivers that would attract a variety of individuals: the adventurous explorer, the serious naturalist, and the family boater. As each stream was paddled and researched, we tried to select key qualities that best described its appeal—for instance, the wild and scenic beauty of the Loxahatchee River. In addition, we looked for any other significant features that might be of interest, such as natural and cultural history. We tried to combine all of these elements into an informative description of the waterways which any interested individual could study while planning a future trip.

For each river covered in this guide, we have included a subjective rating of paddling difficulty and scenic beauty. We have indicated the Department of Transportation county maps on which the river appears, as well as which U.S. Geological Survey Topo Quads (and nautical charts, if needed) can be used for navigation. Finally, while visiting each stream we scouted nearby roads and studied local maps in order to select the most convenient travel routes to the available access points.

We are two enthusiastic canoe paddlers with a great love and respect for Florida's natural beauty; and we know, without question, that there are countless others who share this feeling. We only hope that this book helps you discover more adventure and excitement on the water. So pack your gear, load your boat, and go paddling. Hope to meet you on the river someday.

# How to Use This Book

The information is presented here in a manner designed to assist the paddler with pre-trip planning and, possibly, on-river navigation. The overall descriptions at the beginning of each river are provided mainly to highlight key natural features and interesting historical notes—items that are not usually critical but are still useful in trip selection. The remainder of the stream information is provided in the following format:

## Section Title

Each waterway has been separated into multiple sections, the divisions depending mainly on the location of convenient access points. The title of each section generally includes the names of some geographical features (roads, bridges, parks, etc.) associated with these points, as well as the distance in river miles between the points. In addition, each access has been assigned a letter identifier, which corresponds to a location labeled on the maps accompanying each write-up. The trip follows the letters as they ascend alphabetically. In some cases, a letter designator is used on the maps to indicate an alternate access point or a location that could be mistaken for one. Finally, the maps also include a special symbol Ⓝ which indicates a turnaround point on an out-and-back trip.

## Difficulty

This subjective classification indicates whether that section of river is a breeze to paddle or will require a herculean effort to complete.

No generally recognized difficulty ratings have been established for flatwater wilderness paddling. This guide rates streams according to three levels of difficulty: easy, moderate, and difficult. These ratings apply to average water level conditions. A prolonged drought or the torrential rains of a tropical storm can turn a normally easy paddle into a physical challenge.

3

Easy            Little or no current and a channel free of
                obstructions. Suitable for beginners.
                Average physical stamina is adequate.

Moderate        Noticeable current, some sharp turns, and
                a few obstructions. A knowledge of basic
                maneuvering strokes and better-
                than-average physical stamina are
                prerequisites.

Strenuous       A physical challenge. Swift current, sharp
                turns, and many obstructions demand a
                high level of paddling skill and stamina.

## Scenery

This, too, is a subjective classification, included in this guide to
prepare the paddler for major eyesores as much as for natural
wonders. The subtle beauty of a saltwater marsh may not be
instantly appreciated by paddlers new to Florida's waters. The
following ratings are an overall evaluation of an entire section of a
stream. Don't pass up the lower-rated streams. These usually have
stretches with high scenic value that make the trip rewarding.

Outstanding     The highest level of Florida wilderness.
                An unaltered environment of great
                natural and aesthetic value.

Excellent       Prime Florida wilderness. A paddling trip
                generally free of the intrusions of
                civilization.

Good            Some development along the way but still
                an enjoyable paddle.

Fair            Development and litter detract from the
                wilderness experience.

Poor            Almost total loss of the natural stream
                environment. Severe incursions of
                development along the way.

## County

This indicates on which Department of Transportation county maps the river appears. These maps are quite valuable in locating access points and selecting shuttle routes. A set of maps is contained in a large-format book entitled *Florida County Maps and Recreational Guide*, which is available at most in-state bookstores. The maps may also be ordered from the state government at the following address: Florida Department of Transportation, Map and Publication Sales, Mail Station 12, 605 Suwannee Street, Tallahassee, FL 32399-0450; (850) 414-4050; www.dot.state.fl.us.

## Topo Quads

United States Geological Survey Topographic Quadrangles (phew!) are the preferred maps to use for river navigation. They show most conspicuous landmarks, major river meanders and features of the nearby terrain. Although most streams in this book can be paddled without benefit of the topos, we find that they are quite useful for charting your progress and getting a general feel for the "lay of the land." The specified maps are 7.5 arc-minute quads and are available at most map stores or from the U.S. government at the following address: Mapping Distribution, U.S. Geological Survey, Box 25286, Federal Center, Building 41, Denver CO 80225; (888) 275-8747; http://mapping.usgs.gov.

## Nautical Charts (included only where needed)

These maps come in handy for navigation in and around coastal estuaries and bays, especially for paddling in the Everglades. They show water obstacles as well as local depth indications. They are available from most marinas and map stores or can be ordered at the following address: Distribution Division (N/ACC3), National Ocean Service, 6501 Lafayette Avenue, Riverdale, MD 20737-1199; (800) 638-8975.

*Tall cypresses shade the Upper Econlockhatchee.*

## Access

This describes a convenient route to the put-in point for the given section of river, which is also the take-out point for the previous section. The county maps are useful for locating the desired roads as well as searching for other possible shuttle routes. (In order to condense this information into a small space, the following abbreviations were used: CR for county road, and SR for state road.)

## Trip Description

This section describes major landmarks and other interesting features that the paddler might see along the river. Areas with multiple river channels, swamps, and other areas that might become confusing are also highlighted. Mileage specified in this section is relatively accurate; it was measured by the authors from the appropriate topo quads, using a set of high-quality drafting dividers. The span on the dividers was set using the scale at the bottom of the topos. Typically, this was set for 0.1 mile, but for very twisty streams, 0.05 mile was used.

# Tips for Paddlers

### Weather

The climate in central and south Florida is essentially subtropical in nature. It is marked by high temperatures, an abundance of rain, and high relative humidity. In the winter season, arctic cold fronts sometimes sweep down on the panhandle and send the temperature plummeting. Generally, these fronts dissipate or veer off before they reach the lower peninsula; therefore, the temperatures in that region remain moderate. It is not uncommon, though, for central Florida to experience short periods of near-freezing weather, especially in late December and January. Since these periods are usually associated with cold fronts, paddlers have ample warning of their impending arrival—time to make preparations. For cold-weather paddling, layered clothing helps control body temperature. At night, care should be exercised to ensure warmth around the campsite.

Most problems associated with temperature in central and south Florida occur in the summer when the sun reaches the apex of its journey north. Average maximum temperatures climb into the low nineties and the relative humidity can easily exceed 90 percent. This creates a potentially hazardous combination for the unprepared. The paddler should guard against heat stress and dehydration by drinking plenty of fluids and avoiding overexertion in the heat of the day. Water is the ideal drink; alcohol should be avoided as it reduces the body's ability to dissipate internal heat.

Overexposure to the sun is another pitfall. Sunburn is not only painful; in extreme cases it can be dangerous. Even on overcast days, enough ultraviolet radiation can penetrate to cause a severe sunburn, so precautions are in order. Wearing a wide-brimmed hat and sufficient clothing are good measures, as is using a lotion with a high sun-protection factor.

Rain is another dominant feature of Florida weather. In the central and southern peninsula, the maximum rainfall occurs during the summer months from June through October, and the majority of this activity is associated with thunderstorms. Generally, these storms strike coastal areas early in the afternoon and the interior regions later in the day. High winds, hail and lightning are all potential dangers. Rainfall during the winter season is usually caused by frontal activity and can continue for days.

## Camping and Picnicking

*Public access.* Camping or enjoying a leisurely lunch on the banks of one of Florida's beautiful streams is an integral part of canoeing or kayaking. Unfortunately, many streamside property owners have had unpleasant experiences with poachers, rustlers, vandals and generally messy boaters. Consequently, paddlers will discover a large amount of posted land along the streams of this book. Florida law grants public access up to the mean high-water mark; however, the best policy is to be polite and move on rather than argue the point with a property owner.

*Camping tips.* The water in all of the streams in this book is suspect for human consumption. Either carry along all drinking water or process the stream water to make it safe. Camping supply stores can provide advice on mechanical and chemical treatment techniques. Mosquitoes can be fierce at night, so a bug-proof shelter is recommended. Select a campsite on well-drained ground with good elevation. Sudden torrential rainstorms can flood low areas and significantly raise stream levels. Nearby roads and lots of trash may indicate a popular spot for nighttime carousers. Practice no-trace camping by dismantling fire rings and carrying out all trash. Help maintain water quality by locating latrines well back from the stream and by not using soap in the stream. Use a collapsible bucket and do all washing back from the stream. Several books have been published on the topic of canoe camping, so check libraries and bookstores for more information on this subject.

## Insects and Wildlife

*Insects.* Paddlers can expect harassment by mosquitoes and an assortment of biting flies, especially during the warmer months. Be prepared and take along insect repellent. Look out for wasp nests in low branches overhanging a stream. Wasps become very aggravated when disturbed.

*Alligators.* Everybody thinks of alligators when they think of Florida streams. The alligator has made a remarkable comeback in recent years, and resides on all of the streams in this book. Fortunately, most alligators have a natural fear of people and will slip into the water and disappear as paddlers approach. Florida law prohibits feeding or molesting these animals. (Feeding alligators causes them to lose their fear of humans.)

A strong point must be made about canoeing with dogs. Alligators consider dogs a gourmet food item, so the presence of a dog will attract them. The quick and agile alligator has little trouble taking a dog, even on the shore.

*Snakes.* Three species of poisonous snakes are found in central and south Florida. They are the cottonmouth, coral snake, and eastern diamondback rattlesnake. The cottonmouth (also known as water moccasin) is of most concern to paddlers. The cottonmouth frequently lounges on deadfall trees, and its coloration makes it difficult to spot. Paddlers should exercise caution when negotiating downed trees or making portages. The coral snake and diamondback are most apt to be found near campsites, especially around logs and thick brush.

*Morning on the Alafia near Lithia Springs*

*Doug Sphar takes a rest stop along the Middle Econlockhatchee River.*

## River Access

*Roads.* Most of the put-ins and take-outs listed in this book are on paved roads. A few are on improved dirt roads, but no access points are listed that require four-wheel drive or other special vehicles.

*Unattended vehicles.* A vehicle parked overnight in a remote and unattended location stands a strong chance of being vandalized. Check with fish camps and liveries, as many of these provide shuttle service and a safe place to park. Also, nearby all-night businesses sometimes allow overnighters to park in their lots. Be sure to ask permission. When parking for day-trips, it is better to leave the vehicle near the road rather than back in the woods out of sight.

# Natural History

Few places in the United States can provide the rich and varied paddling experiences that are available in central and south Florida. Less than a day's drive separates the beauty and solitude of the Everglades from the stretches of whitewater on the Hillsborough River. Dark and mysterious cypress forests, high pine-covered bluffs, and the open expanse of a coastal marsh can all be experienced in a single day of paddling. The unique natural history of the lower half of the Florida peninsula makes this enjoyable paddling possible. For the purposes of this book, the lower half of the Florida peninsula has been partitioned into four regions: the Atlantic Coast, the Southwest Gulf Coast, the Central Highlands, and the Everglades. The rivers and streams within each of these regions share generally similar geology and natural communities.

## Atlantic Coast

The streams of the Atlantic Coast drain a long narrow region that was ocean floor until recent geological times. The ancient dune line forms a ridge that isolates the coastal drainage from the St. Johns river drainage. The low elevation of this region—less than 50 feet above sea level—means generally sluggish stream flow. As these streams approach the ocean, they develop broad funnel-shaped mouths known as estuaries.

An estuary is where fresh water mixes with saltwater and ocean tides assume control of the water dynamics. The estuaries of Florida's central Atlantic Coast feature grassy marshes, whereas mangrove swamps are characteristic of the southern Atlantic Coast. The upstream plant communities are often hardwood swamp forests with cypresses, oaks, and maples, or cabbage palm hammocks with palms, oaks, and wax myrtles.

Alligators and otters are frequently seen upstream, but the manatee enjoys the estuary. The estuaries also provide great birding. The heron, egret, anhinga and osprey are at home here. Ducks fly in when the weather turns cold up north.

*Alligator relaxing in Turkey Creek*

## Southwest Gulf Coast

The Southwest Gulf Coast has a number of major stream systems that pierce the interior of the peninsula. Tampa Bay alone is the terminus of four major streams: the Hillsborough, Alafia, Manatee, and Little Manatee. The nearby Peace River constitutes one of the largest drainage basins of Florida. A notable feature of the streams of the Southwest Gulf Coast is an underlying layer of limestone. On streams such as the Hillsborough and Alafia, this limestone spices up a day of paddling with stretches of whitewater. Streams of the region typically have origins in interior highlands and upland plains. These areas are generally characterized by pine flatwoods and palmetto prairies; however, hardwood swamp forests with oak and cypress often are found in the immediate stream valley.

A diverse selection of wildlife unfolds along the way. The distinctive call of the pileated woodpecker is frequently heard as is the knocking noise it makes pecking for insects. The shadowy form of the owl is seen fluttering through the forest canopy. Limpkins and ibis feed in the marshes and swamps that the streams pass through.

*Mixed hardwood swamp on the Hillsborough River*

**Central Highlands**

A region of highlands and upland plains lies north of Lake Okeechobee and inland between the two coasts. The streams in this region drain lands that in some places exceed 150 feet above sea level—stratospheric by Florida standards. This beautiful countryside presents a completely different image of Florida from the palm-studded beach scenes of tourist brochures. Central Highlands forests are comprised mostly of southern pines, but there are areas where oak and hickory predominate.

Fleeting glimpses of deer darting through brush are not uncommon and wild turkey can sometimes be seen. Curious raccoons and playful otters, as well as alligators, make a living along these streams. Groups of turtles basking on downed tree trunks slide into the water as a canoe glides by.

**The Everglades**

There is only one Everglades. A unique combination of ancient events created this wonderful ecosystem—an environment that

*Scenic oak hammock on Arbuckle Creek*

exists nowhere else on this planet. In fact, the Everglades is an International Biosphere Reserve and a World Heritage Site.

The Everglades is a sheet of water that flows imperceptibly south from Lake Okeechobee into Florida Bay. The underlying base of this drainage is a plain of oolitic limestone which was formed from the sediment of an early sea. The gradient of this plain is so gentle that water only drops 15 feet over the hundred-mile journey to Florida Bay.

The limestone is covered with peat soils that support the vast freshwater sawgrass marshes for which the Everglades is famous. Along the coastal extreme of the Everglades, grass prairies give way to mangrove forests. The western extreme of the Everglades has vast stands of cypress forest known as "strands."

*Red mangroves line Nine Mile Pond (Everglades National Park).*

The Everglades is justly famous for birdlife, and early in this century the Everglades supported a plumage industry that decimated many wading bird species. Fortunately, enlightened regulations and changing fashions brought this practice to an end. The Everglades is home for rare and endangered animals. The crocodile and Florida panther are making a last stand here. This unique habitat also supports the Everglades kite, reddish egret, roseate spoonbill, Florida mangrove cuckoo, and Everglades mink.

# Part I:
# Rivers of the
# Atlantic Coast

# Bulow Creek

Bulow Creek is a trip back into Florida history as well as an opportunity to explore a coastal marsh. The put-in is near Ormond Beach at the Bulow Plantation State Historic Site. This site is a relic of the early 1800s when a number of sugar plantations dotted the Florida Atlantic coast. These plantations were burned and abandoned during the Second Seminole War. Paddlers should take the opportunity to visit the old sugar mill and other ruins. There are also nature trails that are worth exploring. Bulow Plantation and the adjacent Bulow Creek State Park form a substantial portion of the west bank of upper Bulow Creek. The park is noteworthy for its rich stand of hardwood hammock.

Bulow Creek originates in Graham Swamp, approximately 3.5 miles upstream from Bulow Plantation. The creek is an easy 13-mile day-trip starting out at the Plantation, going upstream to the origin and then paddling down to the terminus at the Intracoastal Waterway. There is an alternate take-out on Walter Boardman Lane that reduces the trip length to 10.5 miles.

## Bulow Plantation to High Bridge Park (A–C): 13.3 miles

DIFFICULTY: Easy (some deadfalls on the upper section)
SCENERY: Good
COUNTIES: Flagler, Volusia
TOPO QUADS: Flagler Beach East, Flagler Beach West

ACCESS: Bulow Plantation is north of Ormond Beach on SR 5A. This road parallels I-95 to the east and is accessible via the Old Dixie Highway or SR 100 exits on I-95.

TRIP DESCRIPTION: Bulow Creek flows lazily in a general north to south direction. Bulow Plantation is located at the transition between the cabbage palm hammock that lines upper Bulow Creek and the grassy coastal marsh of lower Bulow Creek. Paddling upstream from the Plantation, it is immediately apparent that the creek is afflicted with hydrilla. Floating masses of this aquatic plant restrict paddling to a narrow clear channel. A series

18

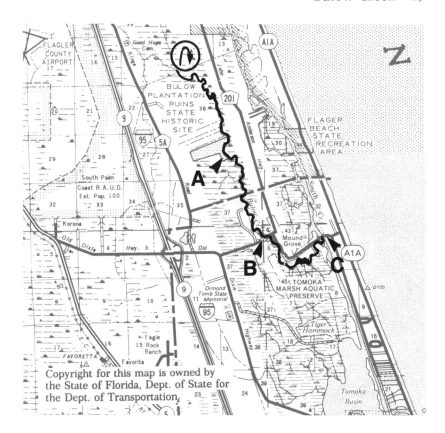

Copyright for this map is owned by the State of Florida, Dept. of State for the Dept. of Transportation.

of five canals enters on the left, evidently the legacy of an abandoned development scheme. Farther upstream, the grassy marsh is gradually succeeded by a narrower stream with margins overhung with palms and swamp hardwoods. A fair number of osprey nests can be seen along this stretch of Bulow Creek, making paddling especially rewarding during spring when the ospreys are building the nests and feeding their young.

At 3.5 miles upstream from the Plantation, the snags and deadfalls of Graham Swamp make further progress difficult and most paddlers will head back downstream. Going south from Bulow Plantation, the creek flows through a broad, grassy coastal marsh. A stream enters from the right at 0.8 mile, as does a canal at 1.5 miles. You reach a large grassy island at 1.8 miles with the main channel going to the right. The alternate take-out on Walter Boardman Lane is located at 3.5 miles. Another mile of paddling and a channel branches off to the right. This is the natural Bulow channel. The straight-ahead channel is a man-made shortcut to the Intracoastal Waterway. The natural channel meanders almost two miles to reach the Waterway, whereas the man-made channel is less than 1.5 miles to the same point. Paddlers taking the natural channel should turn right where the stream again intersects the man-made channel at 0.2 mile from the take-out.

TAKE-OUT (C): High Bridge Park is reached by exiting I-95 onto Old Dixie Highway and driving east one mile and then turning left onto Walter Boardman Lane and driving 0.8 mile to the alternate take-out at (B). Drive another 0.2 mile and then right onto Highbridge Road, which follows Bulow Creek to High Bridge Park.

# Tomoka River

The north-flowing Tomoka River drains a narrow coastal region between the Halifax River lagoon and the St. Johns valley. The Tomoka provides a diverse paddling experience. The upper river is narrow and flows between tall cypress; in contrast, the lower river is broad and flows through the open expanse of a coastal marsh. A substantial portion of the lower Tomoka is within Tomoka State Park. The Timucuan Indian town at the site of the park prompted early Spanish explorers to name the stream *Rio de Timucas* (River of the Timucuans). Later settlers corrupted *Timucas* to Tomoka.

## State Road 40 Upstream (A) and Return: 3.4 miles

DIFFICULTY: Moderate (liftovers)
SCENERY: Outstanding
COUNTY: Volusia
TOPO QUADS: Daytona Beach, Ormond Beach

ACCESS: The SR 40 Tomoka River bridge is less than one-half mile west of I-95 and four miles west of US 1 in Ormond Beach. The put-in is on the southwest approach to the bridge.

TRIP DESCRIPTION: The paddling upstream starts out leisurely because the Tomoka is sufficiently wide and deep to keep deadfalls from being a problem. Old bridge pilings appear one-half mile upstream. Priest Branch, a major side stream, comes in from the right at one mile and is worth taking the time to explore. Upstream of Priest Branch, the Tomoka narrows and flows beneath a tall, dense cypress canopy that suffuses the stream with dim light. The effect is occasionally enhanced by the call of owls that inhabit the area.

The first deadfall is soon encountered and powerboats are effectively denied further upstream access. The stream banks are typical swamp terrain with black mucky soil; however, a hundred feet or so on either side the terrain sharply gains elevation. The distance upstream that can be reasonably paddled will depend on

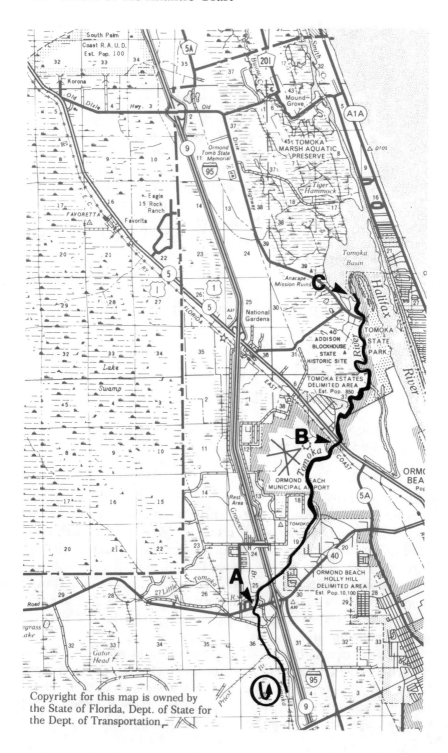

the water level, but eventually the stream becomes choked with deadfalls.

### State Road 40 to US 1 (A–B): 4.5 miles

DIFFICULTY: Easy
SCENERY: Fair
COUNTY: Volusia
TOPO QUAD: Ormond Beach

ACCESS: The SR 40 Tomoka River bridge is less than one-half mile west of I-95 and four miles west of US 1 in Ormond Beach.

TRIP DESCRIPTION: Heading north from the SR 40 bridge, the paddler passes a series of canals into a residential subdivision. Grover Branch enters on the left as the Tomoka makes a turn to the northeast and passes under I-95. The river now becomes broad, and the banks are predominately lined with tall palm trees. A large number of these palms have toppled into the water, and many are submerged only a few inches below the surface. Canoes easily clear most of these trees, but powerboats must stay farther

*Cedar grove along a Tomoka side stream*

out in the channel—a welcome benefit for paddlers. Numerous osprey nests are located along the Tomoka and these birds may be seen performing their household chores.

A little over a mile downstream, the Tomoka divides to pass around a long, skinny island that is nearly a mile in length. Continuing on downriver, a stream enters from the left 0.2 mile before the river passes under a railroad bridge. The US 1 bridge is only another 0.1 mile downstream.

## US 1 to Tomoka State Park (B–C): 4.2 miles

DIFFICULTY: Easy
SCENERY: Good
COUNTY: Volusia
TOPO QUAD: Ormond Beach

ACCESS: The put-in is at the US 1 bridge, 2.5 miles north of the SR 40 intersection with US 1. The only access is via a private marina that charges a small fee for launching.

TRIP DESCRIPTION: There is no observable stream flow on this section of the Tomoka. Considerable residential development is in place on the left bank for the first mile downstream. The Tomoka flows through a broad coastal marsh for most of the distance to the park. The natural character of the marsh has been altered by a large number of mosquito-control canals cut back into the marsh. Most of the shoreline through the marsh is unsuitable for going ashore, but at 2.5 miles there is a stretch of sandy beach and pine trees. A large side stream enters from the right at three miles. The sandy, cedar-covered banks of this side stream provide a welcome contrast to the lower Tomoka marsh. Continuing down the Tomoka, the paddler comes to a highway bridge, and park facilities are among the oaks on the right bank. It is only another half-mile from the bridge to the small cove that houses the park boat ramp and docks.

TAKE-OUT (C): Tomoka State Park is reached by driving east on SR 40 through Ormond Beach and then turning north on Beach Street. This is the last street before crossing the Halifax River bridge. Continue three miles north to the park entrance.

# Spruce Creek

Spruce Creek is noted for the high-forested bluffs that line the upper section of the stream. The high bluffs are an attractive target for development; but, fortunately, a mile-and-a-half stretch of Spruce Creek will become part of a new state park. As the creek nears its mouth at the Halifax River lagoon, it forms a broad estuary known as Strickland Bay, at its confluence with Turnbull Creek. Spruce Creek offers a lazy day of paddling down a broad, slow-moving stream with no obstacles to negotiate. Very low highway and railroad bridges near the mouth deny access to all but small powerboats—a blessing for canoeists and kayakers.

*Bluffs of Upper Spruce Creek*

25

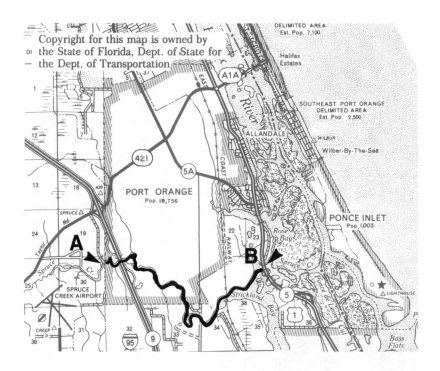

## Airport Road to US 1 (A–B): 6.1 miles

DIFFICULTY: Easy
SCENERY: Good
COUNTY: Volusia
TOPO QUADS: New Smyrna Beach, Samsula

ACCESS: The origins of Spruce Creek are west of Port Orange, a small town immediately south of Daytona Beach. Take the Port Orange exit of I-95 and head west 0.1 mile. Turn south onto Airport Road and drive 1.2 miles to the put-in at the bridge.

TRIP DESCRIPTION: Spruce Creek meanders to the coast within the confines of a bluff-lined drainage. Upon embarking downstream from the Airport Road bridge, the paddler enters the grassy marsh that forms the floor of the drainage. Except on the outside radius of sharp meanders, it is usually impossible to get to the banks of the stream, so most of the trip will be without benefit of shade.

The I-95 bridges will be encountered at one-half mile downstream. There is residential construction upon the north bluff, but it has been discreetly integrated into the oaks and magnolias atop the bluff.

A side stream comes in from the south at two miles downstream. It is possible to paddle half a mile or so up this scenic stream, and the densely wooded banks provide a welcome interlude of shade. A very pronounced horseshoe bend is between the 3.0- and 3.5-mile points. A narrow channel to the left offers a shortcut that eliminates over one-half mile of the trip. Those taking the long way around the bend will skirt the most imposing bluffs seen on the trip. A power line crosses the stream at four miles as Spruce Creek enters Strickland Bay.

The bay becomes quite wide after passing under a railroad bridge at five miles. The north shore of the bay should be favored to avoid inadvertently entering Turnbull Bay—a large body of water that enters from the south. Numerous shallow areas in Strickland Bay are covered with shellfish. These razor-sharp shells can wreak havoc on canoe bottoms or the bare feet of waders. The US 1 bridges become visible soon after passing under the railroad bridge.

TAKE-OUT (B): The take-out is at the US 1 bridge over Strickland Bay. Drive 2.5 miles east on Taylor Road to SR 5A, then turn right on SR 5A and proceed another 2.5 miles to US 1. Turn south on US 1 and drive one mile to Strickland Bay. Note that Rose Bay will be crossed before reaching Strickland Bay. The crossing of Strickland Bay consists of three bridges and two islands. Park off the road on one of the islands.

# Turkey Creek

Turkey Creek provides a pleasant morning of canoeing that includes an opportunity to explore a nature sanctuary. Lower Turkey Creek flows through a hardwood swamp which puts on a fall display of reds, yellows, and oranges. The upper portion of the creek winds through the hammocks and high sandy bluffs of Turkey Creek Sanctuary Park. A canoe landing at the park provides access to a network of interpretive nature trails.

### Pollak Park (A) to Turkey Creek Sanctuary Park and Return: 4 miles

DIFFICULTY: Moderate (deadfalls and sharp turns)
SCENERY: Good
COUNTY: Brevard
TOPO QUAD: Melbourne East

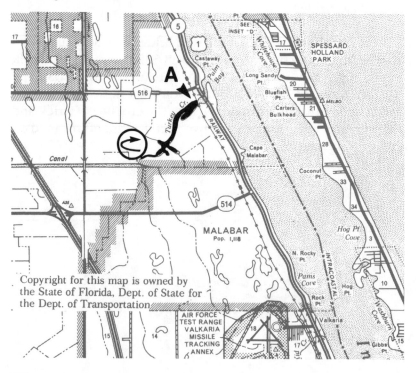

Copyright for this map is owned by the State of Florida, Dept. of State for the Dept. of Transportation

*Bluffs along Turkey Creek*

ACCESS: From US 1 in Palm Bay, drive west on Palm Bay Road. After crossing the railroad tracks, turn left on Main and enter Pollak Park.

TRIP DESCRIPTION: The trip upstream commences in the estuarine mouth of Turkey Creek at the Indian River lagoon and proceeds through a broad region of braided channels. The central channels through Willow Swamp are recommended to avoid the residential development on the north and south banks. Waterfowl are plentiful, and manatees are occasionally seen.

The main drainage of Turkey Creek trends to the southwest and passes under a highway bridge at 1.25 miles from Pollak Park. The character of the stream changes dramatically upstream from the bridge as the residential development is left behind. The channel narrows and the flow quickens as the stream winds through dimly lit forest. The canoeist should be alert for the numerous submerged deadfalls along this stretch of the creek. Precipitous sandy bluffs are encountered at the upper reach of the stream. At 1.75 miles upstream, the sanctuary canoe landing is seen on the right. At 0.25 mile upstream from the canoe landing further progress is blocked by a water-control structure and chain-link fence.

# Sebastian Creek

Sebastian Creek is a three-prong system. The North Prong and South Prong share a common mouth into the Indian River lagoon with a man-made flood-control canal. Aside from sharing a common mouth, the two natural prongs are distinct in character.

The shorter and narrower North Prong sets a serpentine southerly course through thick vegetation that at times resembles a tunnel. A pleasant weekend of paddling is offered by camping at Donald McDonald Park and paddling the prongs on alternate days. This rustic campground is maintained by the State of Florida Division of Forestry and is in a sand-pine forest near the confluence of the North and South prongs. The South Prong meanders north behind the coastal ridge that separates it from the Indian River. Sluggish stream flow and a wide channel provide an easy day of paddling. Large oaks hang out from steep but accessible banks.

## North Prong

### US 1 Upstream (A) and Return: 7.0 miles

DIFFICULTY: Easy
SCENERY: Excellent
COUNTY: Brevard
TOPO QUAD: Grant

ACCESS: A put-in at the US 1 bridge over Sebastian Creek is possible; however, many paddlers prefer to pay a small fee and launch at the marina on the northwest side of the bridge.

TRIP DESCRIPTION: The trip starts in the large, bay-like mouth of Sebastian Creek. Paddlers should follow the north shore 2.2 miles upstream to the entrance of the North Prong. The railroad bridge is 1.0 mile upstream and a large island close to shore is at 1.3 miles. The narrow north channel around the island is the best route on windy days. The narrow entrance to the North Prong is encountered about the time man-made canal structures come into view. You have missed the turnoff if you arrive at the face of a water-control dam.

The intimate nature of the little North Prong is a welcome contrast to the open expanse of Sebastian Bay. The narrow stream meanders through dense vegetation, with a variety of water birds along the way. There are several choke points where paddlers must negotiate tree branches that almost block the way. The North Prong is like a tunnel through the vegetation at its upper extreme. The paddler will eventually reach a point where the water is too low or the vegetation too dense for further upstream travel.

*North Prong of Sebastian Creek near Sebastian Bay*

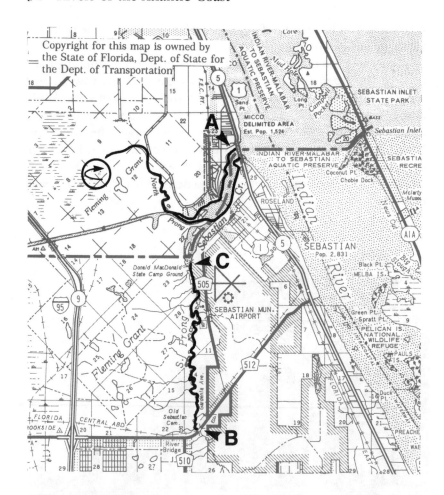

# South Prong

## County Road 512 to Dale Wimbrow Park (B–C): 4.5 miles

DIFFICULTY: Easy
SCENERY: Excellent
COUNTY: Indian River
TOPO QUADS: Fellsmere, Sebastian

ACCESS: The put-in for the South Prong is accessed from either I-95 or US 1. Take the CR 512 exit when coming by I-95 and drive 2.5 miles east to the bridge. To get to the bridge from US 1 in the town of Sebastian, drive 6.5 miles west on CR 512.

TRIP DESCRIPTION: The South Prong starts out narrow and sections of the channel are tree-shrouded. A large tree is down across the stream just short of the bridge but canoes can be pulled under during normal water. Paddlers should be alert to submerged deadfalls during the first 1.5 miles—especially while negotiating the switchbacks. There is some residential development at 1.5 miles downstream where a boat dock with pavilion juts into the stream.

The South Prong opens up below the two-mile point. The meanders become tortuous and in some places the stream nearly doubles back on itself. Banks are low and accessible with cabbage palms and oaks leaning out to provide roosts for anhingas and herons. The South Prong has numerous dead-end false channels awaiting the unwary paddler. A compass and the topographic maps are helpful in avoiding these cul-de-sacs.

The South Prong widens several hundred feet as it nears Dale Wimbrow Park. The very steep north bank ranges from 5 to 15 feet high. A grove of Australian pines on a high bluff contains the stone foundations of an old homestead and indicates that Dale

*Large oaks jut out over South Prong of Sebastian Creek.*

Wimbrow Park is close at hand. The channel into the Dale Wimbrow boat ramp soon appears on the right. Donald McDonald Park is another 0.5 mile downstream.

TAKE-OUT (C): Dale Wimbrow Park is 2.5 miles west of US 1 on CR 505. County Road 505 also intersects CR 512 one mile east of the South Prong bridge. Donald McDonald Park is 0.5 mile east of Dale Wimbrow Park on CR 505.

# St. Lucie River

The North and South Forks of the St. Lucie River form an extensive drainage system that enters the Atlantic Ocean at the coastal city of Stuart. The South Fork has been channelized into the St. Lucie Canal which connects Lake Okeechobee with the Intracoastal Waterway. Fortunately, the North Fork has been designated an Aquatic Preserve, a move that has protected the river and its immediate environs from the burgeoning development that is consuming land in this part of Florida. The upper North Fork flows between banks overhung with large oaks and tall sand pines. Numerous side streams enter the St. Lucie at regular intervals. However, topographic maps reveal these "side streams" to be remnants of oxbows that were short-circuited many years ago. The river below Prima Vista Boulevard is not attractive to paddlers due to the extensive powerboat traffic.

### State Road 712 to Prima Vista Boulevard (A–B): 4 miles

DIFFICULTY: Easy
SCENERY: Fair
COUNTY: St. Lucie
TOPO QUAD: St. Lucie

ACCESS: The put-in is within the southern suburbs of Fort Pierce. Drive west one mile from US 1 on SR 712 (Midway Road). A nicely wooded county park is located at the SR 712 St. Lucie River bridge.

TRIP DESCRIPTION: The St. Lucie flows south from the park through a corridor of high banks covered with large oaks. The main channel is sufficiently wide so deadfalls are not a problem, but obstacles will be encountered on some of the old oxbows.

A triple set of power lines crosses the river 1.5 miles downstream. Paddlers with plenty of time on their hands will want to explore some of the oxbows. Most of these oxbows return to the main channel, but a few are dead-end. At three miles, the river passes through a wide spot that has the appearance of a small

35

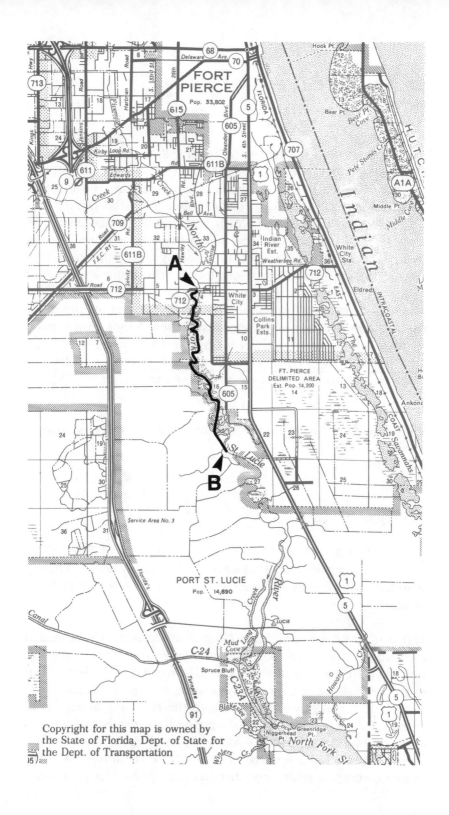

*Old swimming hole on St. Lucie River*

lake. An intersection of five channels with a small island in the center indicates that Prima Vista Boulevard is just 0.1 mile away. The take-out is on the large island formed by the two southernmost channels flowing out of the intersection.

TAKE-OUT (B): To reach the take-out, drive 3.5 miles south from SR 712 on US 1. Turn west on Prima Vista Boulevard in the community of Port St. Lucie. Drive about three-quarters of a mile to a community park that is on a large island in the St. Lucie River.

# Loxahatchee River

The Loxahatchee is the only stream in Florida to be designated a National Wild and Scenic River, and just a few minutes on the stream will convince you that this designation is richly deserved. The upper river is a delight to kayakers and solo canoeists as it zig-zags through a stunningly beautiful cypress swamp. Shortly after entering Jonathan Dickinson State Park, the Loxahatchee changes abruptly as it takes on the sedate character of an estuarine mangrove swamp. It is customary for paddlers to take a lunch break at the Trapper Nelson Interpretive Site. Trapper Nelson, "the wild man of the Loxahatchee," was a locally famous eccentric who developed a unique homestead years ago along the Loxahatchee. Canoe docks, picnic facilities, and drinking water are available at Trapper Nelson's. Park rangers give daily presentations on the wildlife, vegetation and lore of the Trapper Nelson site. *Loxahatchee* translates from early Indian as "Turtle River."

## River Bend Park to Jonathan Dickinson State Park (A–B): 6.5 miles

DIFFICULTY: Moderate
SCENERY: Outstanding
COUNTIES: Palm Beach, Martin
TOPO QUAD: Rood

ACCESS: River Bend Park is west of Jupiter on SR 706 (also known as Indiantown Road). The park is 4.5 miles west of US 1 and one mile west of the Jupiter exit of Florida's Turnpike.

TRIP DESCRIPTION: Soon after leaving River Bend Park, moderately fast water will sweep the paddler into a cypress forest. Adept maneuvering is required to dodge cypress knees and negotiate the sharp turns. Approximately 0.1 mile past the SR 706 bridge, a carry-over ramp traverses an old dam. Dappled sunlight filters through the canopy of the tall cypresses that line the Loxahatchee. Strangler fig entwines many of the cypresses, and pond apple trees are seen. Since this section of river has no true banks,

38

there are few opportunities to go ashore before reaching Trapper Nelson's.

An Indian mound lies back from the east bank at 1.2 miles. A low concrete dam at 1.3 miles is provided with a carry-over ramp. This dam has a drop of about two feet and, during normal water conditions, most people paddle straight over the top. Florida's Turnpike and I-95 bridges are encountered at 1.5 miles. Trapper Nelson's dock is a welcome sight at the halfway point.

Soon after leaving Trapper Nelson's, there is an abrupt transition from cypress forest to mangrove swamp. The Loxahatchee broadens, and current becomes imperceptible as the river comes under tidal influence. High wind sometimes presents a challenge on this stretch. Cypress Creek enters from the left at 3.3 miles, as does Kitching Creek at 3.6 miles. Nearing the 5.5-mile point, the smaller channel to the right will short-circuit a half-mile oxbow.

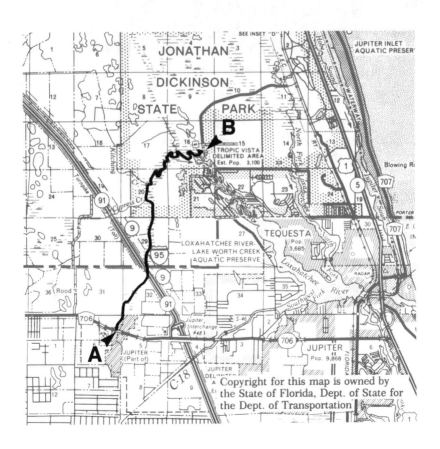

*Lou Glaros on Loxahatchee River*

Soon, a power line crosses the river. The Jonathan Dickinson public boat ramp is up the short channel to the left immediately upstream of the power line.

TAKE-OUT (B): The trip ends at the public boat ramp in Jonathan Dickinson State Park. The park entrance is 1.2 miles north of the intersection of SR 706 and US 1 in Jupiter. The park opens at 8 A.M. It charges a small admission fee, with an additional fee for use of the boat ramp.

# Part II:
# Rivers of the
# Southwest Gulf Coast

# Weeki Wachee River

Florida has approximately 320 springs, which discharge an estimated total of eight billion gallons a day. Twenty-seven of these are first-magnitude springs (discharge of 64.6 million gallons per day or more), greater than any other state in the nation. Of these, many have been left natural and incorporated into state parks or major recreation areas, while others, such as Weeki Wachee, have been developed commercially.

*Downed giant cypress on the Weeki Wachee River*

Weeki Wachee Springs is located west of Brooksville and north of Tampa. It is the source of a river of the same name, which flows for about eight miles through coastal swamp until it empties into the Gulf of Mexico near the small town of Bayport. Bayport was once a major trade center and the Weeki Wachee River was used as a transportation route for barges hauling goods to nearby Brooksville. This ended, though, when the railroad was built through Brooksville.

The name *Weeki Wachee* comes from the Creek Indian language and literally means "little spring" (*Wekiwa chee*). Contrary to its Indian name, it is a major spring and does create a very swift current in the upper six miles of the river. Because there is no public access either at the spring, which is commercially owned and operated, or along the river, which is privately owned, the spring can be reached only by paddling the six miles upstream against the swift current from the closest public access at SR 595. Downstream of that point, the river broadens and slows as it begins to meander through a coastal tidal marsh. As the river approaches the Gulf of Mexico, the current flow becomes dominated by tidal action and the influence of the spring discharge diminishes.

Although several miles of this river are highly developed with shoreline housing and numerous dredged canals, the rest of it retains a wild character and is quite a beautiful place to paddle. However, its high concentration of powerboat traffic on the weekends—especially in summer—makes us recommend it for weekday paddling.

## Bayport Boat Ramp to State Road 595 (A–B): 2 miles

DIFFICULTY: Easy
SCENERY: Fair to excellent
COUNTY: Hernando
TOPO QUAD: Bayport

ACCESS: From the town of Brooksville, travel west on SR 50 for ten miles to the intersection with US 19, which is the location of the Weeki Wachee Springs commercial attraction. Continue west on SR 50 for nine miles, through the town of Bayport, until the road dead-ends at a small park. There is a fishing pier on the south side

of the park, and water access is down a concrete boat ramp into a
canal on the east side.

TRIP DESCRIPTION: After entering the main river channel at the
south end of the access canal, the paddler should turn left (east)
and head inland through the tall grasses of the tidal marsh. This is
the area where the river enters the Gulf of Mexico, and the channel is about 200 yards wide. The fishing is excellent here, and
manatees are frequently seen.

After continuing due east for about three-quarters of a mile past
several large side streams and a few channel markers, the paddler
will turn to the northeast. Shortly, a large sign will show the Mud
River to the northeast and the Weeki Wachee to the east. The Mud
River originates 1.5 miles from this point at Mud River Spring and
makes a very nice trip in its own right. The numerous side creeks
and bays are interesting to explore.

As the Weeki Wachee continues east, it narrows gradually.
Three-quarters of a mile past Mud River begins a residential area.

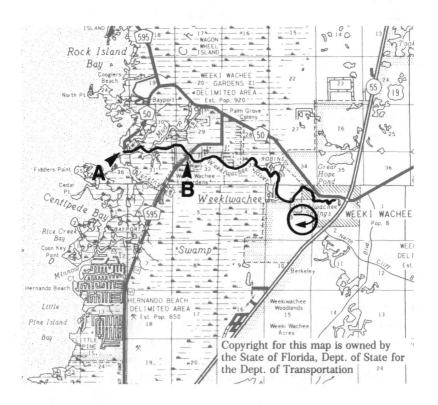

Until reaching the take-out at SR 595, the paddler will travel through dense development, past continuous sea walls and countless boat docks. The take-out is located on the south side of the river just east of the SR 595 bridge. Since the river has narrowed in this area, the current is swifter than before and the paddling more difficult.

## State Road 595 (B) to Weeki Wachee Springs and Return: 12 miles

DIFFICULTY: Strenuous
SCENERY: Fair to excellent
COUNTY: Hernando
TOPO QUADS: Bayport, Weeki Wachee Springs

ACCESS: From the town of Brooksville, travel west on SR 50 for ten miles to the intersection with US 19, where the Weeki Wachee Springs commercial attraction is located. Continue west on SR 50 for 4.5 miles to the intersection with SR 595. Turn left (south) and travel for two miles to the bridge over the Weeki Wachee. The put-in is located in a small park on the southeast side of the bridge. Access is down a concrete boat ramp or grass slope on the park's east side. There is ample parking and restroom facilities on the property.

TRIP DESCRIPTION: On this section of river, the current is quite swift, the severity depending on the local width and depth of the channel. Because of this, the trip upstream to the spring can be very difficult and seemingly endless. Likewise, the return trip, although not requiring much exertion, can still be quite tricky. The swift current and the way it varies across the width of the river, especially at sharp turns, requires careful paddling to avoid careening through the shoreline vegetation or, worse yet, taking an accidental swim.

The put-in is on a long canal that enters the river from the south. From the canal, the paddler will turn to the right (east), away from the bridge, and continue upstream. The first one and a half to two miles of the trip pass through a highly developed area. Concentrated housing on the left (north) is accompanied by a continuous sea wall, numerous dredged canals, and countless

boat docks. The south shore is undeveloped and heavily vegetated.

The remainder of the trip, except for a small area near the halfway point, is undeveloped. In this area, the river traverses the
Weeki Wachee Swamp. Water oaks and some palm trees are inter-
mingled with the cypress, and the observant paddler will likely
see numerous herons, egrets, vultures, and ospreys.

Just past 4.5 miles, an excellent swimming area appears on the
left (north) side. Nearby is a small, privately owned park with a
boat ramp, swimming dock, and rope swing.

Five miles from the put-in, the paddler enters the property
owned by the Weeki Wachee Springs commercial attraction. Just
past it, on the north shore, is the attraction's injured-pelican
recovery area; a short distance farther, in mid-river, is a set of tiny
houses on stilts, which is used to keep a small family of monkeys.
Paddlers should maintain a safe and respectful distance since this
is private property, and the captive animals are wild.

The upstream trip ends just past the loading dock used for the
attraction's sight-seeing boats. Tightly packed with tourists, these
large boats will likely be seen in the latter stages of this trip.

# Hillsborough River

The Hillsborough is a long and diverse river, flowing for nearly 54 miles from the Green Swamp north of Lakeland to Hillsborough Bay in Tampa. It is a river rich with history. Thousands of years ago, the Timucuan and Calusa Indians inhabited the surrounding land, and remnants of their middens and burial mounds can still be found not far from the river. The Seminole Indians, a mixture of northern Creeks and the surviving Calusas, later emerged along the Hillsborough. As American pioneers hungered for Florida land, they came in contact with these tribes; inevitably, the Seminole Wars were ignited. Fort Alabama, now called Fort Foster, was built along the river and remains as a reminder of that bloody conflict. The river was originally named *Lockcha-popka-chiska* (river where one crosses to eat acorns) by the Seminoles, an obvious reference to their love for the large oak trees that line the shores. The British named it after the Earl of Hillsborough, a Colonial Secretary in the 1700s.

*First drop in the State Park Rapids of the Hillsborough River*

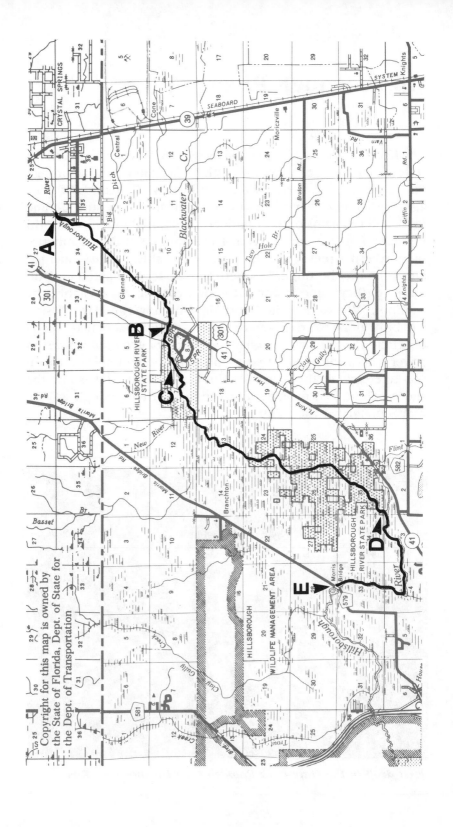

The river is fed by 690 square miles of natural drainage, most of which results from five main tributaries, including Flint and Blackwater creeks. During the wet summer season, rain runoff swells the river while during the dry winter and spring months, the water level is low and maintained primarily by baseflow from Crystal Springs near the Green Swamp headwaters.

As the Hillsborough proceeds southwest toward Tampa Bay, it traverses a variety of terrain, predominantly a mixture of cypress and hardwood forests. The well-known Seventeen Runs area is a mixed hardwood swamp, which contains southern red cedar, cabbage palmetto and cypress. Although the underlying surface in the area is sand and clay, numerous limestone formations in the upper river create frequent mild rapids. About ten miles downstream of the Green Swamp, the river enters Hillsborough River State Park, one of the oldest and largest parks in the state.

## Crystal Springs to Hillsborough River State Park (A–C): 6.2 miles

DIFFICULTY: Moderate
SCENERY: Excellent
COUNTIES: Pasco, Hillsborough
TOPO QUAD: Zephyrhills

ACCESS: From the intersection with SR 54 in Zephyrhills, proceed south on US 301 for two miles to Crystal Springs Road. Bear left (south) onto this road and follow it for 1.5 miles to a very narrow bridge over the river. Crystal Springs Road can also be reached from I-4 east of Tampa by driving north on US 301 for 18 miles. Access is down a slender dirt path on the northeast side of the bridge. Due to loose barbed wire and slippery ground, caution is urged in this area. Vehicles can be left along the road, although the shoulders are narrow and rough. Alternate parking might be arranged one-half mile south of the bridge at a private facility called Crystal Springs Park.

TRIP DESCRIPTION: From the put-in, turn right and proceed downstream. The first one-quarter mile of this trip is somewhat difficult due to deadfalls, multiple channels, and shallow water. If exiting the boat during pullovers, the paddler should be very cautious of the slippery, sharp limestone rock along the riverbed.

A man-made waterfall on the left marks the entrance to Crystal Springs Park. For the next several miles, the river water is sparklingly clear and flows swiftly through flat ranchland lined with a thick forest of oaks, cypress, and palms. The river has a sand bottom with numerous limestone formations and, in many places, the water racing over the limestone creates small whitewater rapids. Occasionally, the paddler will also encounter deadfalls or other major obstructions, which must be carried over.

Blackwater Creek enters the Hillsborough about 3.7 miles from the put-in. Three-quarters of a mile later, the river passes under a wooden bridge and Fort Foster appears on the left. At this point, US 301 spans the river at what is called Burnt Bridge (B), which provides no access to the river from the road.

About one mile past the bridge, the paddler will encounter the State Park Rapids, a 150-yard stretch of river with three Class II drops separated by smooth water. Each drop is accented by a cluster of limestone rocks and standing waves. The first and third drops are best paddled on the left, while the safest route for the second set is along the right. The rapids can also be portaged along a footpath on the left.

Within one-half mile of the rapids, the paddler will pass a wooden bridge and then the state park's canoe concession. The public take-out is around the next left turn in the river, on the left up a shallow dirt slope.

## Hillsborough River State Park to Flint Creek Wilderness Park (C–D): 6.7 miles

DIFFICULTY: Moderate to strenuous
SCENERY: Outstanding
COUNTY: Hillsborough
TOPO QUADS: Zephyrhills, Wesley Chapel, Thonotosassa

ACCESS: From I-4 east of Tampa, drive north on US 301 for 13.5 miles to the entrance of Hillsborough River State Park. This point can also be reached from SR 54 in Zephyrhills by traveling south on US 301 for seven miles. Once inside the park, follow the loop road to the canoe-launch area. There is an entrance fee.

*Paddling near the end of Seventeen Runs on the Hillsborough River*

TRIP DESCRIPTION: This section of the Hillsborough contains the well-known Seventeen Runs, an area of cypress swamp where the river branches into numerous swift, shallow creeks. The entrance to the Runs is about three miles downstream of the put-in. Prior to that point, the river channel is broad and the current slow as it traverses a forest thick with oak, cypress, pine, and cedar. The water is darkly stained by the tannin seeping from the surrounding land, and it obscures the occasional limestone rock embedded in the sand bottom.

Just before the beginning of Seventeen Runs, a rustic home, a wooden bridge, and a small group park will be passed on the left shore. Shortly thereafter, a fork appears in the river and the main current seems to go right; however, the paddler should bear left and carry-over or portage around a large hyacinth jam, which marks the beginning of the Runs.

Over the next several miles, the paddler will encounter numerous deadfalls, some of which may need to be carried over, depending on the water level. The river continues to separate into multiple branches, most being impassable due to shallow bottoms, or what appears to be an endless series of major obstructions. A general rule in Seventeen Runs is to bear left, except at a major righthand turn located about one-half mile (or 20 minutes' travel time) past the entrance. At this point, a red reflector, which may be covered during very high water, directs the paddler along a channel which branches off at an angle greater than 90 degrees. At very low water, both channels are obstructed by deadfalls.

For the most part, the terrain in this area is thick with tree roots, leaf litter, deadfall and some poison ivy. Very few places are clear enough for going ashore. In the last mile of this section, the river gradually broadens and the current slows.

The end of the section is marked by the appearance of a wooden boardwalk. At this point, Flint Creek enters from the left and the Hillsborough continues on to the right. The take-out is reached by paddling straight ahead past the boardwalk and into a narrow canal leading into the Flint Creek Wilderness Park.

### Flint Creek Wilderness Park to Morris Bridge County Park (D–E): 3.5 miles

DIFFICULTY: Easy
SCENERY: Outstanding
COUNTY: Hillsborough
TOPO QUAD: Thonotosassa

ACCESS: From I-4 east of Tampa, drive north on US 301 for eight miles to the entrance of Flint Creek Wilderness Park, which is on the left side. This point can also be reached by traveling east of I-75 on Fowler Avenue for 1.5 miles to the intersection with US 301. Bear left onto US 301 and continue for 3.5 miles to the park entrance. The park has adequate parking and good restroom facilities.

TRIP DESCRIPTION: Access at this point is down a gentle slope into a small basin. From here, proceed north down a short, narrow canal, and past a boardwalk on the right. The canal ends at the confluence of Flint Creek and the Hillsborough River. At this point, the paddler should turn left and proceed downstream.

For the next several miles, the journey is quite pleasant. An

*Expect some carry-overs in Seventeen Runs on the Hillsborough River.*

occasional deadfall will be encountered, and although these may require a carry-over, they may also block powerboats from using this section of river. The channel is broad and the water slow-moving as it passes through a tropical landscape of cypresses, oaks, and palms. At any given time, hundreds of white ibis might inhabit this area and treat the canoeist to a special show as they swoop through the trees en masse, filling the air with the sporadic drumming sound of wing beats.

At about two miles, the river turns north and continues in that general direction for the remainder of this section. As the sunlight filters through the dense forest foliage, it creates a patchwork of bright green hues contrasted with deep shadows.

At the end of this section, the river passes beneath Morris Bridge. The take-out is at a small county park on the left just past the bridge. Access to the park is at a wooden dock or up a grass slope.

TAKE-OUT (E): Morris Bridge County Park is reached by traveling east of I-75 on Fletcher Avenue. Eventually, this road becomes Morris Bridge Road; about three miles past I-75, it crosses over the Hillsborough River. The county park is on the northwest approach to the bridge. Ample parking is available.

# Alafia River

The Alafia River (pronounced AL-uh-FYE) extends for about 45 miles from meager beginnings near the town of Mulberry until it widens into a substantial waterway and empties into Hillsborough Bay near Riverview. The north prong flows east to west through the gently rolling hills of the Polk uplands and the flatwood forests of the Gulf coastal lowlands. During periods of unusually heavy rainfall the Alafia River basin sustains very high water flow rates, although its average discharge rate is not high enough to rank it as a major Florida coastal river. In its upper reaches, the river passes through cattleland and near phosphate mines; though these contribute to high nutrient concentrations and low dissolved oxygen levels, the Alafia retains a fair water quality.

The section of the Alafia covered in this guide extends for 26 miles from the Keysville Bridge in east Hillsborough County to the Alafia boat ramp in a residential area of the town of Riverview. The section above Keysville Bridge is not included because it is shallow, narrow, and not readily accessible. Below the boat ramp, the river widens substantially and, although it can be paddled, it is not recommended because of a large volume of powerboat traffic. Between these points, the Alafia is moderately swift and, at numerous places, small formations of riverbed limestone have created short whitewater rapids. It meanders through beautiful oak canopies and past areas heavily vegetated with cypress trees, cabbage palms, and palmettos. Although wildlife is not abundant on this river, the observant paddler may see numerous bird species, opossum, raccoons, cattle, and, possibly, an alligator relaxing on the riverside.

The river passes through two county parks: Alderman's Ford and Lithia Springs. Lithia Springs has swimming, restrooms, shower facilities, and a developed camping area. Alderman's Ford has restrooms, a very nice nature walk along boardwalks and dirt trails, and a primitive camping area.

Located within 35 miles of the greater Tampa area and serviced by numerous canoe liveries, the Alafia is a popular river. Certain sections of it can be quite crowded on weekends, especially during the summer. However, on weekdays it is quiet and the paddler

54

*The Alafia meanders through a gnarled upland forest.*

may be alone on the whole river. The Alafia's popularity is also evident in the moderate amount of trash littering the water and its banks.

### Keysville Bridge to Alderman's Ford County Park (A–B): 7 miles

DIFFICULTY: Easy to moderate (some obstructions may require liftovers or portaging; several short whitewater rapids)
SCENERY: Fair
COUNTY: Hillsborough
TOPO QUADS: Nichols, Keysville, Lithia

ACCESS: From the SR 39 exit on I-4 in Plant City, travel south on SR 39 for 10.5 miles to the intersection with CR 676. Turn left (east) on this road and proceed 1.5 miles to the Keysville Bridge, which will be reached just after the road turns sharply to the south. Access is below the overpass, down a small dirt path on the northwest side of the bridge.

From Tampa, take SR 60 east to the intersection with SR 39 just south of Plant City. Turn right (south) and drive for 3.5 miles to CR 676. Proceed as above.

TRIP DESCRIPTION: From the put-in, turn right and proceed downstream. For the first few miles, the river meanders through heavily vegetated landscape. In this section, the Alafia flows past nearby strip mines and cattleland, but these are not readily observable since the banks are high on both sides. However, a barbwire fence is easily seen on the right. Eventually, the bank reaches a height of 30 to 40 feet, giving the river landscape a mountainlike quality.

Two and a half miles downstream from the put-in point, the river flows beneath a railroad trestle, turns to the right and carries over a 30-yard stretch of very mild rapids. The Alafia enters

*Playing the rapids on the Alafia River*

Alderman's Ford County Park one and one-half miles later. In this area, cypress trees are abundant and the sides of the river are heavily vegetated.

About 1.5 miles past the entrance to Alderman's Ford, the river narrows to 10 or 15 feet and the south prong enters from the left. Approximately one-half mile later, the river flows beneath a footbridge, widens again, and passes under SR 39. Just before another footbridge crosses the river, a channel flows in sharply from the left. This channel leads to the take-out point, a nice wooden dock located 100 yards upstream on the right.

This section of the Alafia is quite secluded: the paddler will likely not see another person until Alderman's Ford. However, there are signs of civilization (some garbage, barbwire fence, etc.), and the beautiful scenery does not occur until the last couple of miles of the run.

## Alderman's Ford County Park to Lithia Springs County Park (B–D): 11.5 miles

DIFFICULTY: Easy to moderate (several short whitewater rapids)
SCENERY: Good
COUNTY: Hillsborough
TOPO QUADS: Lithia, Dover

ACCESS: From the SR 39 exit on I-4 in Plant City, travel south on SR 39 for 12 miles to Alderman's Ford County Park on the left. Proceed about one-half mile farther south past the Alafia River bridge and turn right (west) on Thompson Road. A short distance farther on the right will be the gated entrance to the canoe-launch area of Alderman's Ford. Follow the signs to the parking and unloading area. Restroom facilities are available. River access is down a paved walkway under a footbridge. This park is open only from 8 A.M. until sunset, so plan shuttles accordingly. There is no charge to enter this park.

TRIP DESCRIPTION: While the section of the Alafia from Keysville Bridge to Alderman's Ford is generally secluded, this section of river tends to be quite crowded. On weekends, it is a very popular area and is serviced by three canoe liveries. However, on weekdays it is quiet and the paddler may be alone on the river. The

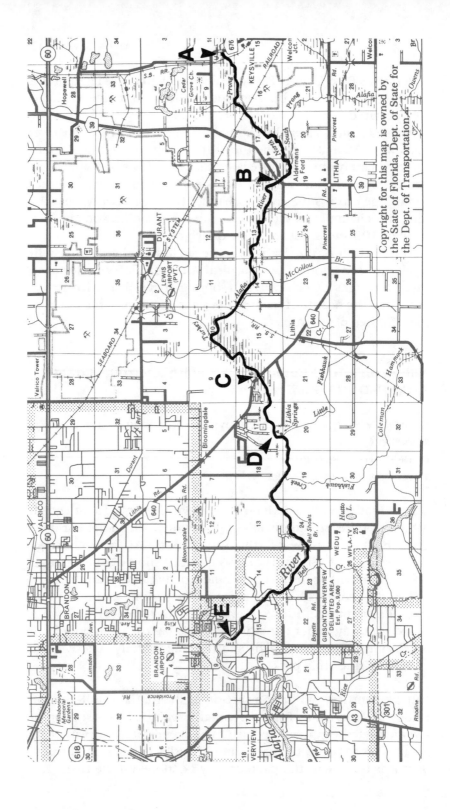

popularity of this section is also evident in the moderate amount of trash littering the river and its banks. This offsets the otherwise scenic beauty of the landscape.

The Alderman's Ford canoe-launch area is on a side channel off the main river. Proceed to the left from the wooden dock, and about 100 yards downstream make a gradual left turn onto the Alafia. At this point, the river passes beneath a footbridge, part of the county park boardwalk system. In the next quarter-mile, the river turns from due north to west to east and then begins a general westerly flow direction.

This section of the Alafia meanders through beautiful oak and cypress woodlands, and good campsites are relatively abundant. The banks are occasionally four to five feet high, increasing the difficulty of landing a canoe and unloading gear. In most places, though, the shoreline is shallow and sandy. There is private property along the river, so be sure to respect the property rights of others when selecting a camping or picnicking site.

Between Alderman's Ford and Lithia Springs, there are at least six sets of mild whitewater rapids. At low-water levels, some of these become impassable because of exposed rocks and require a portage or carry-over. The first of these occurs approximately 1.5 miles downstream from Alderman's Ford and the rest are spaced at irregular intervals.

At 5.5 miles, the river flows past a gouged-out area of forest. There is a sloped bank of white sand and a rickety-looking brick structure on each side. These are the remnants of an old railroad trestle that was disassembled years ago; it is not a safe place to stop for picnicking or camping.

At 9.5 miles, the Alafia passes beneath CR 640. A clearing on the right just past the bridge can be used as an alternate access point (C). It is reached from Alderman's Ford by traveling south on SR 39 for one mile, turning right (west) on CR 640 and proceeding for four miles to the Alafia River bridge. Access is down a short paved road on the northwest side of the bridge. One-quarter mile farther downstream, on the right, are the docks for two of the local canoe liveries. These also are good access points (for a fee); they are reached by land by traveling just over 0.1 mile west of the CR 640 bridge.

The take-out at Lithia Springs County Park is 1.5 miles past the CR 640 bridge. At this point, the river is flowing southwest and turning to the northwest. Just past the take-out, a large white pipe crosses the river about 30 feet above the water. The take-out is up a small rise on the left.

## Lithia Springs County Park to Alafia Boat Ramp (D–E): 7.5 miles

DIFFICULTY: Easy
SCENERY: Good
COUNTY: Hillsborough
TOPO QUADS: Lithia, Riverview, Brandon

ACCESS: From the SR 39 exit on I-4 in Plant City, travel south on SR 39 for 13.5 miles to the intersection with CR 640 (Lithia-Pinecrest Road) in Lithia. Turn right (west) and proceed for 2.5 miles to Lithia Springs Road. Turn left (west-southwest) and travel 1.5 miles to the county park. From Tampa, proceed east on SR 60 to CR 640. Turn right (southeast) and travel 5.5 miles to the bridge over the Alafia River. Go one-half mile past the bridge to Lithia Springs Road and proceed as above. A small entrance fee will be charged for every person to enter the park. The park is open only from 8 A.M. till sunset, so plan shuttles accordingly. Access to the river is at a canoe-launch area on the right side of the perimeter road.

TRIP DESCRIPTION: The first three miles of this section contain some of the most scenic landscape on the entire Alafia. Huge oaks line high banks and the tree canopy shades up to 75 percent of the river area. The shore is heavily vegetated with palmettos and numerous varieties of ferns and vines.

The current is moderately swift, and creates several sets of whitewater rapids as it flows over limestone rock formations. There are countless overhanging trees and branches which can snag the unwary paddler, especially when negotiating a tight turn.

From the put-in, the paddler passes beneath a large overhead pipe and swings around the county park on the left. At 0.4 mile, the Lithia Springs basin, which is the park swimming area, empties into the Alafia. The tannin-stained water is mixed with silt and dirt, and when it meets the crystal-clear discharge from the spring it creates a very noticeable contrast line.

Just past Lithia Springs, Little Fishhawk Creek enters the river from the south, and one mile later Fishhawk Creek enters also from the south. Except at low-water level, both can be paddled, although Little Fishhawk Creek is extremely narrow.

Four miles downstream of the put-in, the Alafia passes beneath Bell Shoals Bridge and, from this point on, the shoreline becomes highly developed. The river broadens and becomes quite slug-gish. For the next 3.5 miles to the take-out, the paddler will likely encounter much powerboat traffic. The take-out is on the right (east) side of the river at a concrete boat ramp lined with high retaining walls.

TAKE-OUT (E): The Alafia boat ramp is located in residential Riverview. From Lithia Springs County Park, follow Lithia Springs Road for 1.5 miles to CR 640. Turn left, travel three miles, and turn left again onto Bloomingdale Road. Proceed for three miles, turn left (south) onto King Street, and go 0.8 mile to Center Street. Turn right and continue until the road dead-ends at the boat ramp.

# Little Manatee River

If you paddle the Little Manatee River in the dry winter months, you will encounter a shallow, narrow waterway enclosed by steep banks, heavily vegetated with oaks, pines, willows, and an occasional cedar. High above, the trees form a thick canopy that shades most of the river and, below, numerous small beaches will invite you to stop and enjoy a refreshing swim. Unfortunately, the low water will also expose the eyesore of the river—the occasional piece of discarded furniture or the heap of unsightly trash.

If you paddle this river in the wet summer season, though, its character will be remarkably different. High water will cover a large number of the swimming beaches and, during periods of recent heavy rainfall, the swift current will race the paddler through the branches of the overhead tree canopy. During times of especially high precipitation, it is best to avoid the section of the river upstream (east) of US 301 and remain in the downstream area, where the riverbed broadens and is not subject to rapid water-level fluctuations.

For about 40 miles, the Little Manatee stretches across southern Hillsborough County from its origin as a tight twisting creek near Fort Lonesome and Wimauma, until it broadens and empties into Tampa Bay near Ruskin. In 1982, a large segment of the river was classified by the state as Outstanding Florida Waters, a designation that grants the Little Manatee special protection against water pollution. Additionally, the Little Manatee State Recreation Area has been opened. This 1600-acre park is located along the south shore of the river west of US 301 and should provide further protection from development.

This guide includes the 16-mile section from Leonard Lee Road south of Wimauma to 24th Street near Ruskin.


## Leonard Lee Road to County Road 579 (A–B): 3.5 miles

DIFFICULTY: Moderate
SCENERY: Good
COUNTY: Hillsborough
TOPO QUAD: Wimauma

ACCESS: From US 301 in Sun City Center, proceed east on SR 674 for four miles, through the town of Wimauma. Turn right (south) on Leonard Lee Road and continue on this graded lane for 2.5 miles to the narrow, unrailed bridge over the river. Access is down a gentle grass slope next to the bridge. The grassy shoulders are broad enough to leave vehicles safely along the road.

TRIP DESCRIPTION: This is the wildest section of the river and the most difficult to paddle at high water. The narrow channel causes rapid water-level fluctuations after heavy rainfall, and the gradient of the riverbed produces a swift current, which can propel the paddler through snags and overhanging tree branches. This section is also the site of a drop in the riverbed which, while unnoticeable at high water, creates a small waterfall at low water during the dry season. The remainder of this section snakes through tall wooded banks and past a few small, sandy beaches until it flows beneath the bridge at CR 579. The take-out is on the left (east) on the downstream side of the bridge.

*The Orange Blossom Special used this historic railroad bridge on the Little Manatee.*

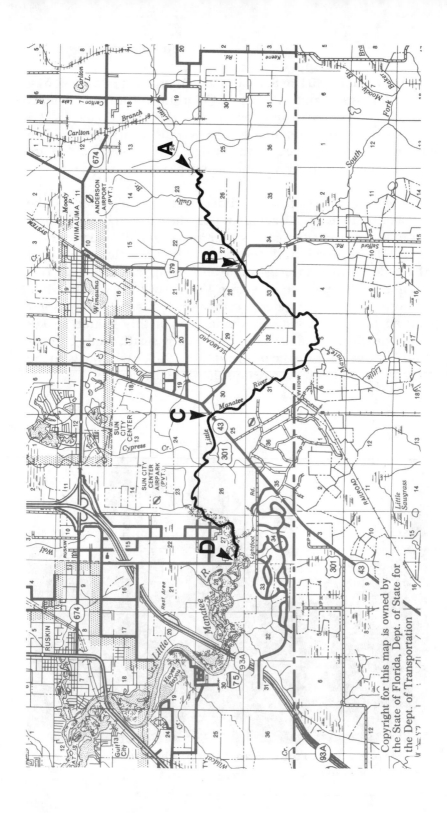

## County Road 579 to US 301 (Canoe Outpost) (B–C): 7 miles

DIFFICULTY: Easy to moderate (at high water)
SCENERY: Good
COUNTIES: Hillsborough, Manatee
TOPO QUAD: Wimauma

ACCESS: From US 301 in Sun City Center, proceed east on SR 674 for 2.5 miles through Wimauma. Turn right (south) on CR 579 and proceed four miles to the bridge over the river which occurs just after the road turns sharply to the east. An alternate route is to proceed south on US 301 for 2.5 miles past SR 674 to Saffold Road, which intersects from the left (east). Turn onto Saffold Road and drive for three miles to the junction with CR 579. Turn right onto CR 579 and proceed one-quarter mile to the bridge. Access is on the southeast side of the bridge down a narrow dirt path, which can be quite slippery when wet. The shoulders of the road are narrow and very rough, so exercise caution when leaving vehicles.

TRIP DESCRIPTION: The first 3.5 miles of this section are much like the previous section. The narrow river snakes its way through tall wooded banks, and the swift current can race to high-water levels when rainfall has been heavy. Oaks and willows line the shore and create an overhead canopy that occasionally opens up as the river widens.

The observable riverside is totally undeveloped except for two major structures. The first, a water intake gate for a local Florida Power Corporation plant, is located just past three miles. It appears quite suddenly through the trees and disappears just as quickly as the river turns sharply to the north and back into the surrounding woods. Less than two miles from here is an old, long-abandoned railroad trestle. This massive brick structure with overhead steel support was built in 1913 and was used by the famous Orange Blossom Special. At low water, sandy beaches are exposed nearby, providing lovely places to stop for a rest.

For the last half of the trip, the river broadens gradually and the tree canopy gives way to more open areas. There are fewer deadfalls and obstructions to negotiate, and the channel does not wind as much as it does upstream. The take-out at the Canoe Outpost is located just downstream of the US 301 bridge on the south side of the river.

## US 301 (Canoe Outpost) to 24th Street (C–D): 5 miles

DIFFICULTY: Easy
SCENERY: Fair
COUNTY: Hillsborough
TOPO QUADS: Wimauma, Ruskin

ACCESS: From SR 674 in Sun City Center, proceed south on US 301 for three miles to the bridge over the river. Just south of this, on the west side of the road, is a gravel drive marked by a wooden sign for Canoe Outpost. Follow the drive into the parking area. Access to the river is down a small, muddy slope near a wooden dock, and there is a nominal launching fee. This local canoe livery is an excellent site to leave vehicles. For a small charge the proprietors, a very friendly and helpful young couple, will arrange shuttle service to any of the access points for the Little Manatee.

TRIP DESCRIPTION: The first three miles of this section are quite pleasant as the river meanders gently through a pretty, wooded area which includes the Little Manatee State Recreation Area on the south shore. The first mile has numerous overhangs and obstructions, which must be carefully negotiated, but it clears up beyond that. Past three miles, the river broadens to about 150 feet and becomes shallow and slow, while house-and-trailer development begins to appear on the right (north). The take-out is located on the north shore just past the only set of power lines, resembling telephone wires, that crosses the river. The take-out is up an asphalt street ramp that appears to dead-end in the river.

TAKE-OUT (D): From Sun City Center, travel west on SR 674 for four miles past US 301. One mile west of I-75, turn left (south) onto 24th Street and proceed for three miles until the road dead-ends at the river.

# Manatee River

The Manatee River flows into the Gulf of Mexico and Tampa Bay west of the city of Bradenton after extending for nearly 40 miles through central Manatee County. It is supplied principally from about 150 square miles of watershed and, along its entire length, countless creeks drain their contents into it. The river traverses the Gulf Coastal Lowlands, and the surrounding area is marked by pine flatwoods, sandhills, and hammock communities.

Historically, the land was used for cattle-grazing, farming, and harvesting timber, and many of the local coniferous trees were also used for turpentine production. Later, east of what is now the city of Bradenton, numerous small communities were quickly developed and almost as quickly disappeared. Rye was at the eastern end of a commercial boat-traffic route that originated in Bradenton; and Manhattan was an early planned-area subdivision development that eventually went bankrupt, and whose tax deeds were sold to the Rutland Ranch.

*Steep, forested banks border the Upper Manatee River.*

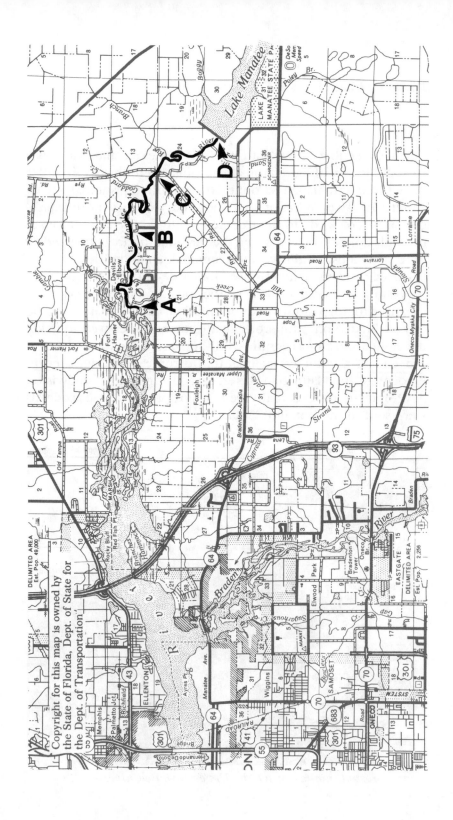

In the 1960s, a dam was constructed on the river and Lake Manatee was formed. This 2400-acre reservoir provides potable water for Sarasota and Manatee counties and is also part of the Lake Manatee State Recreation Area, which offers boating, swimming, and camping. The dam gates are opened at irregular intervals to release overflow into the river, especially after heavy rains. In the narrow river channel near the dam, the discharge from the lake can raise the water level several feet an hour. The opening of the gates is announced well in advance by a series of siren blasts from the dam structure.

The section of river covered in this guide extends for 6.5 miles from the dam to the confluence with Gamble Creek. There are three main access points. The Rye Road bridge put-in is two miles downstream from the dam, Ray's Canoe Hideaway is four miles, and Aquatel Lodge is six miles. The latter two are privately owned and require a launch fee, but do provide a secure place to leave a vehicle. The bridge put-in is public, but is the least secure place to park.

## Aquatel Lodge to Lake Manatee Dam (A–D): 6.5 miles

DIFFICULTY: Easy to moderate (if paddling upstream while dam gates are open)
SCENERY: Good
COUNTY: Manatee
TOPO QUADS: Parrish, Rye, Verna

ACCESS: All three access points are located east of Bradenton on Upper Manatee River Road, which enters SR 64 (Bradenton-Arcadia Road) from the north, 2.5 miles east of I-75.

To reach the put-in at Aquatel Lodge (A), drive for 3.5 miles on Upper Manatee River Road to the intersection with Aquatel Road, which is marked with a small sign for the lodge. Turn left (north) onto this dirt road and proceed for about one-half mile. The entrance to the lodge is on the left, and the dirt road continues ahead. There are rental cottages and RV pull-in sites on the property, as well as ample parking. Access is down a dirt-and-grass ramp on the river or down a concrete ramp into a small bay just off the river.

To reach the put-in at Ray's Canoe Hideaway (B), proceed 1.5

miles east of Aquatel Road on Upper Manatee River Road. Turn
left (north) on Hagle Park Road and drive through a small subdivision. When this road ends, turn left onto a dirt drive and follow it
into Ray's Canoe Hideaway. For a small fee, canoes can be
launched down a brick ramp. There is a large grass parking area
and restrooms on the property.

The Rye Road bridge (C) is one mile east of Hagle Park Road
where Upper Manatee River Road ends and crosses Rye Road,
which is graded. The best access is on the southeast side of the
bridge at a small sandy beach. There are areas to park on the south
side of the bridge.

TRIP DESCRIPTION: Because of the nature of this river, point-to-
point trips will not be described. Instead, we will highlight key
features and how they relate to the various access points. The dam
can be reached only by paddling upstream from any of the access
points. If the gates have been opened, the current will be swift,
especially near the dam. In spite of these conditions, round-trips,
even from Aquatel Lodge, are possible; in fact, they make an
excellent day-trip.

Downstream of Aquatel are two side streams worth taking for
short trips. Mill Creek enters the Manatee from the south a short
distance east of the lodge, and Gamble Creek enters from the
north just downstream from there. Gamble Creek meanders for
several miles through tall grasses typical of coastal marshes and is
composed of numerous mazelike braided channels. Paddling on
the Manatee downstream of the confluence with Gamble Creek is
not recommended due to powerboat traffic.

Between Aquatel Lodge and the Canoe Hideaway, the river is
broad and sluggish. The north shoreline is undeveloped and vegetated with marsh grasses, palms, and some oaks, while the south
shore has scattered homes and a large privately developed area
called Christian Retreat Campground. Devils Elbow, a conspicuous meander in the river west of the retreat, is located one-half
mile upstream of Aquatel.

East of Ray's Canoe Hideaway, the riverbed begins to narrow
and bluffs gradually appear on the sides. Some of these are bare
sand bluffs that drop into pleasant beaches ideal for rest stops.
One of these is located on the south shoreline near the Flying
Eagle Boy Scout Camp, just upstream of a double-switchback in

the river. There are several others between the Rye Road bridge and the dam.

East of the bridge, the bluffs are higher, with tall sand pines growing on them. Only an occasional building or trailer can be seen through the thick vegetation, to mar the fine scenery in this area.

If the dam gates are open, the roar of the rushing water can be heard at least a mile away. As the dam is neared, the paddler might encounter patches of discolored foam. This is formed as the water bubbles over the spillway at the foot of the dam. Due to swift current and possible obstructions, the paddler should not approach the dam too closely.

# Braden River

The city of Bradenton, located in west central Florida on the Gulf coast, grew up around the sugar plantation of wealthy landowner Dr. Joseph A. Braden, who developed the land during the Civil War. Braden-town was situated at the confluence of the Manatee and Braden Rivers and, therefore, had a major influence on the development of budding communities located inland. The area is steeped in historical tradition. Hernando de Soto landed there in 1539 at an area commemorated by DeSoto National Monument; he later made contact with the peaceful Timucuan Indians at an

*Resting near wooded bluffs along the Braden River*

72

ancient village and ceremonial site now called Madira Bickel Mound.

The Braden River extends for about 25 miles from its headwaters in a central Manatee County watershed to its confluence with the Manatee River in Bradenton. At its start, the river flows east. It is tight and densely vegetated but broadens gradually as numerous side streams enter it. After passing beneath I-75, it turns north and widens considerably. Along its entire length, the Braden has a very sluggish current and is shallow in many places. Local legend has it that, during a major hurricane, Hector Braden (Joseph's brother) and his horse drowned in quicksand at one of these shallow crossings while taking a shortcut back to the sugar plantation.

Because of considerable powerboat traffic and lack of good access on the broad, wide-open section of the Braden downstream of Jiggs Landing Fish Camp, this guide covers the river only upstream of that point. Although powerboats will still be encountered, the paddler will generally find the local boaters and fishermen to be very friendly and polite. Paddling upstream from Jiggs Landing is quite easy due to the sluggish current; an excellent day- or overnight-trip can be enjoyed by continuing past Linger Lodge (an alternate access point) into the remote area where the river snakes through high forested bluffs, and beautiful campsites abound.

### Jiggs Landing to Linger Lodge (A–B): 4.5 miles

DIFFICULTY: Easy
SCENERY: Fair
COUNTY: Manatee
TOPO QUAD: Lorraine

ACCESS: From I-75, proceed west toward Bradenton on SR 70 for 1.5 miles to the intersection with Braden River Road. From Bradenton, this road is reached by traveling east on SR 70 and proceeding one mile past the Braden River bridge. The official sign for this road is quite small, so a more definite indication of the turnoff is a large white sign for Linger Lodge on the south side of the road. Turn south and travel one mile to the entrance to Jiggs Landing, where the road turns sharply to the east. Jiggs Landing is

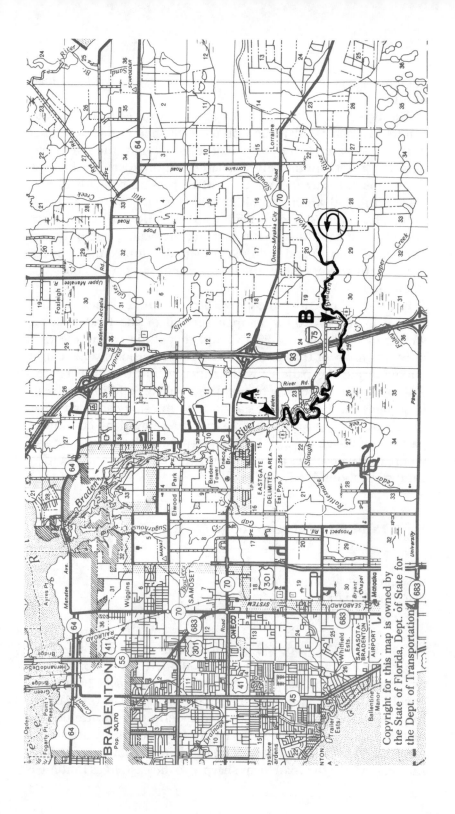

a fish camp with a number of rental cottages, a boat dock, and a small bait shop where a limited choice of groceries and refreshments is available. Access is down a concrete boat ramp, and there is a nominal launching fee.

TRIP DESCRIPTION: The launch point is located on Ward Lake, a half-mile wide expanse of water through which the Braden River flows. The main channel of the river can be reached by proceeding to the left (east) from Jiggs Landing and going around the island on the right. It can also be reached by paddling one-quarter mile due south across Ward Lake to the point where Rattlesnake Slough enters the Braden. (Note: This route does not appear on the DOT county maps or the USGS topographs.) For the first two miles, the river meanders through a residential area. The channel is about 50 yards wide, and there are boat docks and a sea wall along the left (east) shoreline, while the opposite shore is undeveloped. Several small bays branching off the main river are interesting areas to explore, although partially developed.

At 1.5 miles from Jiggs Landing, Cedar Creek enters from the south. This makes a nice side trip, even though it narrows significantly after one-quarter mile. At two miles, while paddling in a southeast direction, the canoeist will encounter a large island. The main riverbed circles this island on the right while a narrow shortcut canal branches off to the left. Just past this, the riverside is undeveloped. The main channel snakes to the east, west, then back east again, and at 2.5 miles a side bay opens up on the right. A short distance later, a power line right-of-way crosses the river. For the remainder of the trip to Linger Lodge, the Braden wanders lazily through scenery typical of this area. Large oaks, cypress, and palms line the river, and amidst the ground vegetation are some nice openings where a paddler can pull over and picnic. Fishing is good in this area; the paddler will likely see numerous powerboats and canoes working the shoreline and bay mouths for bass, bluegill, and other fish.

Just short of four miles, I-75 crosses the Braden. At about 4.5 miles, turn north then east into a region where homes and small boat docks are again seen on the left bank. The Linger Lodge takeout is located at the next elbow where the river turns sharply to the south. Look for the Linger Lodge sign and a concrete access ramp near numerous boat slips. The journey on this section of the Braden is not complete until the paddler saunters up the wooden walkway to the patio tavern, settles in for some refreshments and relaxation, and takes some time to observe the many interesting pieces of hardware and other artifacts that are used for decoration.

## Linger Lodge (B) to Points Upstream and Return: 6–8 miles

DIFFICULTY: Easy
SCENERY: Excellent
COUNTY: Manatee
TOPO QUAD: Lorraine

ACCESS: From Jiggs Landing (see above) proceed east on Braden River Road. This paved road turns south, then east, and about 1.5 miles from Jiggs Landing becomes graded. One and one-half miles later, after passing over I-75, it turns sharply south and leads directly to Linger Lodge. Access is down a concrete ramp near numerous boat slips. There is very limited parking at this point, so it is not recommended as a put-in for large groups.

TRIP DESCRIPTION: The character of the Braden changes upstream of Linger Lodge. Downstream of this point it has been broad and open, considerably developed, and highly utilized by power-boats. Upstream, though, it narrows gradually and begins to snake its way through an upland forest. Furthermore, the occasional shallows created by the shifting river bottom make travel by powerboat difficult and almost impossible at low-water levels.

From the put-in, the paddler should proceed left (south) and follow the riverbed around a sharp left turn. At the elbow of this turn is a small bay into which Cooper Creek flows. Cooper Creek is a tight, twisting, and partially overgrown tributary to the Braden that can be paddled as an interesting side trip. For three-quarters of a mile past Linger Lodge, proceed in a northeast direction; there will be one large double-switchback turn. Some trailers and houses will be visible on the left in this area, but most signs of development will disappear rapidly.

Past this section, the river begins to wind its way east through tall bluffs which gradually appear on both sides. Sand pines and other scrub vegetation on top of the bluffs create a beautifully scenic contrast with the various oaks growing amidst the wild-

*Pleasant camping area on the Upper Braden River*

flowers and grasses in the clearings nearer the water level. In many areas, the vegetation on the bluffs has given way to erosion, leaving large sand faces and, on some of these, exposing the deep roots of tall sand pines.

This section of the Braden is ideal for camping. Between one and three miles past Linger Lodge, campsites are abundant. The areas along the bluffs provide excellent views while the riverside clearings are nestled comfortably among oak hammocks and groves of nut trees. East of this section, finding a suitable camp-site is more difficult due to closely packed vegetation and steep banks. The river is only about 25 feet wide here and quite shallow in many places. Dense vegetation and tree growth create an over-head canopy that blocks most direct sunlight. Depending on the water level, paddling past the four-mile point is questionable; therefore, when numerous shallow areas requiring drag-overs are encountered, the paddler may take this as a sign to turn back for Linger Lodge.

# Ding Darling National Wildlife Refuge

Sanibel and Captiva Islands, located in the Gulf of Mexico across San Carlos Bay from Fort Myers, are reached via the Sanibel Causeway. At one time, these barrier islands were relatively undeveloped, providing a quiet refuge for those seeking solitude or a shell-hunting excursion along the well-known beaches. Development finally came to the islands, however, and rustic terrain gave way to condominiums, hotels, and apartments. Thankfully, the community insisted that the changes be made in step with nature: consequently, the island visitor may still experience a natural setting. In addition, a large section of the islands was designated as the J.N. "Ding" Darling National Wildlife Refuge, and protected from future encroachment.

Vegetated with mangrove and sawgrass, the refuge is the home for a variety of animals including ospreys, moorhens, brown pelicans, and alligators. Winter migration brings an abundance of northern visitors, such as blue-winged teals, pintails, and mergansers, to name a few. Canoeing offers an excellent way to tour the refuge and observe the wildlife, along one of the two established canoe trails.

## Commodore Creek Loop Trail (A): 3 miles

DIFFICULTY: Easy
SCENERY: Excellent
COUNTY: Lee
TOPO QUAD: Sanibel
NAUTICAL CHART: 11427

ACCESS: The Tarpon Bay Marina is reached from the Sanibel Causeway by proceeding west on Periwinkle Way for three miles to the intersection with Sanibel-Captiva Road. Turn right and drive to Tarpon Bay Road. Turn right again and follow this graded road to the marina. The marina offers launch facilities, ample parking, and canoe rentals.

TRIP DESCRIPTION: The Commodore Creek Trail is located at the southeast corner of Tarpon Bay. This marked trail snakes for sev-

78

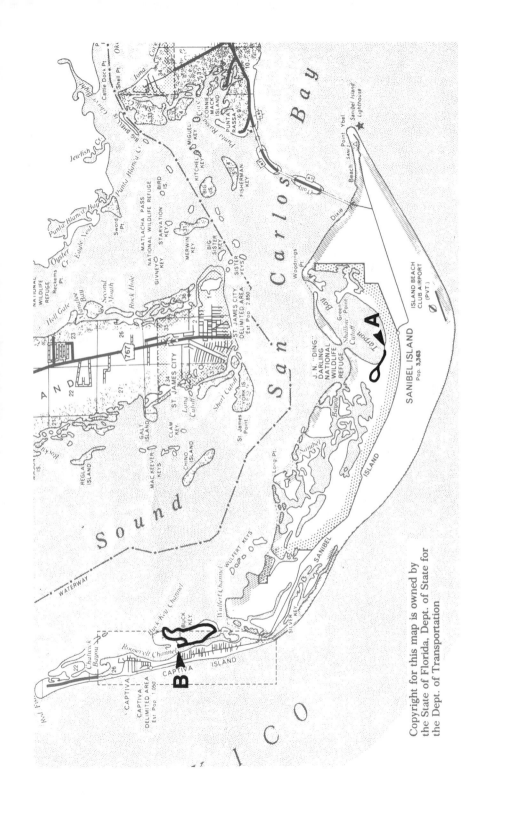

eral miles through tidal mud flats and stands of red mangrove. It offers excellent views of wading birds and small marine animals scurrying along the seabed. The trailhead is reached by paddling three-quarters of a mile west of the Tarpon Bay Marina along the south shore of the bay.

### Buck Key Loop Trail (B): 4 miles

DIFFICULTY: Easy to moderate (at low tide)
SCENERY: Excellent
COUNTY: Lee
TOPO QUADS: Wulfert, Captiva
NAUTICAL CHARTS: 11427

ACCESS: The second refuge canoe trail is on Buck Key, a small island off the east coast of Captiva Island, Sanibel's northern neighbor. The access for this loop trail is at 'Tween Waters Marina on Captiva Island, about nine miles past Tarpon Bay Road on Sanibel-Captiva Road.

TRIP DESCRIPTION: The trailhead is southeast of the marina, about one-quarter mile across Roosevelt Channel. The paddler will first cross Hurricane Bayou, a small bay within Buck Key, which is surrounded by mangrove and is the site of a sunken boat hulk. Dolphins frequently enter the bayou to frolic in the water. Buck Key is heavily vegetated with mangrove and interior hammocks. During the era of Spanish exploration it was inhabited by Calusa Indians who left a group of shell mounds which can still be visited. The canoe trail is part of a canal system that was dug in recent years for mosquito control.

The canal is entered on the north side of Hurricane Bayou and continues for about one mile until it opens up onto Pine Island Sound on the east side of Buck Key. The paddler should turn right and follow the coast for 0.8 mile to the entrance to another canal. Follow this canal for several miles until it intersects Roosevelt Channel. Turn right and follow the channel for about one mile to the marina.

Because of its proximity to the Gulf of Mexico, the water level on this loop trail is related directly to the tides. At low tide, the trail is almost impassable, so the paddler is advised to plan trips accordingly.

# Estero River

Ten miles south of Fort Myers, on the Gulf coast, lies the small community of Estero. Bounded on the west by Estero Bay and on the east by the Corkscrew Swamp, Estero was established in 1894 by a religious visionary from Chicago, Dr. Cyrus Reed Teed. Dr. Teed was the founder of a religion that advocated communal living, communal ownership of property, and celibacy. He called this new religion "Koreshanity," which is derived from *Koresh,* the Hebrew word for Cyrus. Among this religion's most unique beliefs was the theory that the earth was a hollow sphere. Life existed on the inner surface and overlooked the sun, stars, and universe in the center. In 1896, Dr. Teed even conducted an experiment with a simple device, known as a rectilineator, which proved to him that the earth's surface was indeed concave, a central feature of his theory.

The bulk of the Koreshan settlement was built on the Estero River, about five miles upstream from Estero Bay. Although the movement declined after Teed's death in 1908, many of the buildings remain intact and are preserved in the Koreshan State Park, administered by the Florida Department of Natural Resources (DNR). This park, which extends for a mile along the Estero River, has a beautifully wooded camping area, nature trails, a concrete boat ramp and, of course, the historic Koreshan settlement.

*Estero* is a Spanish word meaning "estuary" and was first applied long ago by explorers as they sailed into the bay. Estero Bay is an ecologically rich area in which red mangrove and turtle grass provide a continuous food supply for the large fish population. This productive area has been qualified as a State Aquatic Preserve, and much of the land within two miles south of the Estero River and extending through the park is state-owned and protected.

The section of the Estero River covered in this guide extends for five miles from the point where it passes beneath highway US 41 until it flows into Estero Bay. Along this course, the character of the river changes dramatically, beginning as a narrow waterway channeled by limestone and shaded by large oaks, and eventually broadening as it flows through the Spartina grass and mangrove of the tidal marsh. The flow of the river is affected by the tides, so the paddler may want to check local tide tables while planning a trip, though it is not necessary. Because of extensive powerboat traffic on weekends, the ideal time to paddle this river is through the week.

## US 41 to State Park Boat Ramp (A–B): 1 mile

DIFFICULTY: Easy
SCENERY: Good to excellent
COUNTY: Lee
TOPO QUAD: Estero

ACCESS: From exit 19 on I-75, travel west on Corkscrew Road for two miles to US 41, or Tamiami Trail. Turn right (north) and proceed for one-quarter mile to the bridge over the Estero River. The Estero River Tackle and Canoe Outfitters is located on the northeast side of the bridge. There is ample parking, and boats may be launched from a small wooden dock for a nominal fee.

TRIP DESCRIPTION: From the launch point paddle to the west, beneath the US 41 bridge. Along the entire length of this section,

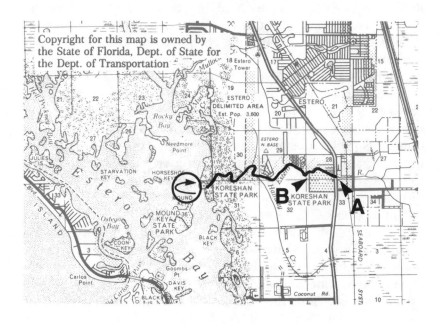

the south shore is in the state park, and for the first one-quarter mile several buildings of the historic Koreshan settlement can be seen through the woods on the left. Although the north shore is developed with several trailer parks, their associated docks and boat slips, the scenery is still quite nice. Large oaks draped with Spanish moss and bromeliads shade most of the river area, and the lush shore vegetation is highlighted with an occasional wild hibiscus. Layers of limestone, stained green in irregular patterns by fungi, and dripping wet from the damp mosses that cling to it, protrude from the riverbanks. It is not uncommon to see an alligator resting on a submerged log or outcropping, its body partially obscured by the dark, tannin-stained water.

The state park boat ramp is concrete and has stone retaining walls. It is on the south side of the river and very easy to find.

## State Park Boat Ramp (B) to Estero Bay and Return: 8.4 miles

DIFFICULTY: Easy
SCENERY: Good to excellent
COUNTY: Lee
TOPO QUAD: Estero

ACCESS: From exit 19 on I-75, travel west on Corkscrew Road for two miles to US 41, or Tamiami Trail. Proceed past the traffic light into Koreshan State Park. There is a small charge to enter the park, with an additional fee to use the boat ramp. Follow the road past the camping area to the ramp. There is a large grass field for parking and a nearby picnic site.

TRIP DESCRIPTION: From the boat ramp, proceed to the left (west) toward Estero Bay. Within two miles of the put-in, the river passes a large trailer park and another residential area, both on the right (north). The channel is about 60 yards wide here, and the south shore is lined with tall Australian pine trees. At 1.5 miles, Halfway Creek enters from the south. This lovely little waterway meanders through a brackish marsh and, in places, separates into multiple channels that weave their way through mangrove and turtle grass. All the vegetation looks alike, so it's easy to become confused; but with a compass and a knowledge of the current direction at the mouth of the creek, the paddler can eventually find the main channel.

Mangrove is the predominant vegetation from Halfway Creek to Estero Bay, although there is also a lot of Spartina grass and, on the high ground, some Australian and sand pines.

One-quarter mile past Halfway Creek, a long narrow bay protrudes to the south-southeast; at its mouth lies the wreckage of a sunken boat. The wheel house is always visible and, at low tide, the bow can be seen angling out of the water. For safety reasons, the hulk should not be approached too closely. The dark tannin-stained water obscures the view, making it difficult to see pieces of hull wreckage which may obstruct the paddler.

From this point on, the river meanders gently to Estero Bay past a number of small bays and side streams, which are interesting areas to explore in their own right. At 3.6 miles, a channel enters the river from the northeast. This side creek winds its way through a thick mangrove forest, and the observant paddler is likely to see herons and egrets perched in the roots, or an osprey soaring overhead.

Just past four miles, the river enters Estero Bay and the influence of the tides becomes quite pronounced. Caution should be exercised in this area, for moderate chop, enough to swamp a canoe, can develop quickly in the bay. Oyster beds, with their sharp damaging shells, are located near some of the mangrove thickets.

Horseshoe crabs can be seen in the water and scurrying along the sand on mangrove islands. Mullet may surprise the paddler as they jump out of the water next to the boat and continue along in a series of airborne arcs. Occasionally, paddlers may notice the ghostly form of a stingray passing underneath.

# Part III:
# Rivers of the
# Central Highlands

# Lake Norris and Blackwater Creek

Blackwater Creek—tight and hauntingly beautiful as it snakes through an ancient, maybe prehistoric, cypress swamp—is thought by many locals to be the "impassable waterway." Born on the waters of Lake Norris, it stretches for over twenty miles, eventually emerging onto the Wekiwa River just upstream from the St. John's River. Many hardy souls have tried to traverse the entire waterway and have met with difficulties—extreme difficulties. The middle section is mined with dead snags hiding in tea-stained low water, and nature has barricaded the lower reaches with countless deadfalls. Past the confluence with Seminole Creek and Sulphur Run, the waterway totally disappears into a myriad of tiny fingers, none large enough to support a canoe, and doesn't reform until just prior to the Wekiwa.

Impassable? Sure! But not to be missed. Just stick to the upper stretch of Blackwater, never wandering more than a few miles

*Paddling past an abundant cypress forest*

from Lake Norris. The channel is deeper and there are fewer obstructions to contend with (except in low-water conditions). The silence of the cypress forest is sometimes hypnotizing, and the mood may only be broken by the passing of an animal resident.

Lake Norris is the jewel of the trip. Guarding the lake from all approaches, the cypress woodlands extend into the water, creating in many places a 150-foot wide buffer—an intriguing area to explore—that plays host to a metropolis for osprey and other birdlife. The adventuresome boater can spend hours investigating the lakeshore, weaving a canoe through the maze of cypress. And, except for one boy scout camp and a few rustic homesites, the surrounding area is a wilderness sanctuary.

## Blackwater Creek Bridge (A) to Lake Norris and Return: 2–7 miles

DIFFICULTY: Easy to moderate (at low water)
SCENERY: Excellent
COUNTY: Lake
TOPO QUAD: Paisley

ACCESS: From Eustis take Orange Avenue (SR 44) to CR 437. Turn left and drive north for 2 miles to the intersection with CR 44A. Turn right and travel 0.5 mile to Lake Norris Road, which is marked by a small grocery store on the northeast corner. Turn left and follow the road for 2.5 miles to the bridge over Blackwater Creek. Access is down a dirt ramp on the northwest approach to the bridge.

TRIP DESCRIPTION: From the bridge, turn left and paddle upstream toward Lake Norris. At moderate to high water conditions, you will encounter very few obstructions, while at lower water you must negotiate a large number of deadfalls and bottom snags. There is a slight current and the meandering streambed creates a lively, challenging slalom course for a paddler. Watch for two sets of ancient wood pilings crossing the creek. They were set years ago for bridge construction. The first is about a half mile from the put-in and the second spans the mouth of the stream that meets Lake Norris.

Lake Norris is a large body of water and wind conditions can kick up sizeable waves, so it's best to paddle around the periphery of the lake. Besides, that's where the gnarled cypress forest grows out of the water, so the scenery is much more tantalizing. For a quick but exciting trip into this forest, paddle along the west side of the lake. Turn around at your discretion or paddle the entire lake shore. Then return to the put-in via Blackwater Creek.

## Blackwater Creek Bridge to CR 44A (A–B): 4 miles

DIFFICULTY: Strenuous
SCENERY: Excellent
COUNTY: Lake
TOPO QUAD: Paisley, Pine Lakes

ACCESS: (Same as above.)

TRIP DESCRIPTION: Beautiful? You bet! Difficult? Absolutely! Fun? That depends upon your tolerance for carry-overs and your skills at boat handling around difficult deadfalls and other obstructions.

From the put-in, turn right and paddle under the bridge. At low water levels, you will encounter obstructions almost immediately. At higher levels, the first mile or so provides almost clear passage. Beware, though, the situation only gets worse as you proceed downstream. Even under the best of conditions, this trip will consume several hours. But, for the adventurous paddler who tackles it, the experience of the enclosed swamp and the solitude that comes with it may well be worth the effort.

TAKEOUT (B): From Eustis, take Orange Avenue (SR 44) to CR 437. Turn left and drive north for 2 miles to the intersection with CR 44A. Turn right and travel for 3.25 miles to the bridge over Blackwater Creek. The best access to the creek is down a vegetated slope on the northwest approach to the bridge.

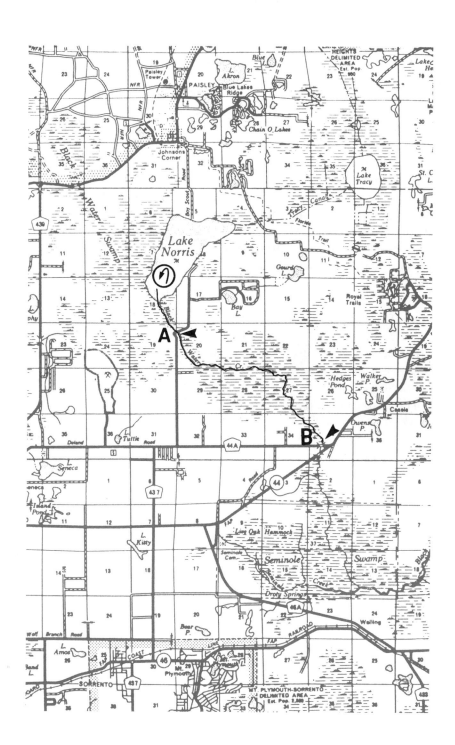

# Econlockhatchee River

The Econlockhatchee River, known to locals as the Econ, is a jewel in the midst of developing Orange and Seminole counties. This beautiful stream has so far escaped the rampant growth that has consumed many of the area's natural attributes. The upper river challenges paddling skills as it winds through the dim light of a mysterious cypress forest. Things are slow and easy on the lower river as the Econ enters the open expanse of the St. Johns valley. Those with a bent for the supernatural may be interested in the glowing "Oviedo Lights": many people claim to have seen them at night above the water, while standing on the CR 419 bridge. This strange luminescent phenomenon has long been part of the local lore of the Econ.

## State Road 50 to County Road 419 (A–B): 8.7 miles

DIFFICULTY: Moderate (strenuous during low water)
SCENERY: Outstanding
COUNTIES: Orange, Seminole
TOPO QUADS: Oviedo SW, Oviedo

ACCESS: The Econlockhatchee passes under SR 50 at 15 miles east of I-4 in Orlando and 20 miles west of I-95 in Titusville on the east coast. There is public access at the bridge, but better facilities are available for a fee at the nearby private park.

TRIP DESCRIPTION: This section of the Econ will bring paddling skill to the fore as sharp turns, cypress knees, deadfalls, and moderately swift current present a challenge. Check on stream conditions before attempting this trip. During low water the number of carry-overs becomes intolerable, and the river can be dangerous after major rainstorms. The towering cypresses keep the stream in perpetual shade, which makes this stretch attractive for summer paddling. The beauty of the cypress forest and the lack of development provide a memorable trip.

Watch for submerged concrete obstacles under the bridge at 1.7 miles. Two power lines will be encountered, one at two miles

*Upper Econlockhatchee River near SR 50*

and another at three miles. The Econ's banks are not very accessible during the early going, but sandy banks appear beyond the six-mile point. A major milestone occurs at the confluence with the Little Econlockhatchee River. From this point, it is only 0.1 mile to the bridge at CR 419.

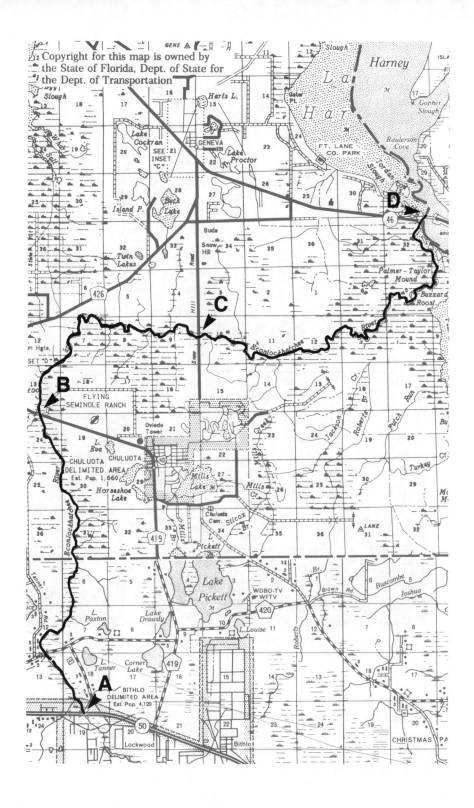

## County Road 419 to Snow Hill Road (B–C): 7.6 miles

DIFFICULTY: Easy
SCENERY: Excellent
COUNTY: Seminole
TOPO QUADS: Oviedo, Geneva

ACCESS: The Econlockhatchee passes under CR 419 between Oviedo and Chuluota. This road runs north from SR 50 about 1.5 miles east of the SR 50 Econlockhatchee bridge. The put-in is at the east end of the bridge.

TRIP DESCRIPTION: The character of this section of the Econ is markedly different from the previous section. The cypress trees give way to hardwoods on high sandy banks. Seasonal wildflowers add color and interest. After the first mile the Econ widens, the current becomes languid, and deadfalls cease to be a problem. Many good campsites are seen, but most are posted, unfortunately. An abandoned railroad trestle spans the river at 1.5 miles from Snow Hill Road. The trestle now supports a footbridge that is part of the Florida Trail System.

## Snow Hill Road to State Road 46 (C–D): 10.1 miles

DIFFICULTY: Easy
SCENERY: Excellent
COUNTY: Seminole
TOPO QUAD: Geneva

ACCESS: Snow Hill Road runs due north from Chuluota to Geneva on SR 46. From US 17-92 in Sanford, drive 14 miles east to the CR 46 intersection in Geneva. Drive south one mile on CR 46 and turn left onto Snow Hill Road. The Econlockhatchee is another four miles south. Access is on the southwest end of the bridge.

TRIP DESCRIPTION: The paddling is easy on this stretch of the Econ. The river is moderately wide, the current slow, and deadfalls are not a problem. The riverbanks are high, sandy, and shaded by oaks during the first eight miles. The extensive posting of "No Trespassing" signs on both banks mars an otherwise ideal camping

*Lou Glaros pausing on the Econlockhatchee River near Snow Hill Road*

stream. The banks become lower as the eight-mile point is passed; and the oaks are replaced first by cabbage palms, and then by grassy prairie as the St. Johns valley is entered.

The Econ merges into the St. Johns River at 9.3 miles. Turn north and paddle toward the SR 46 bridge, visible in the distance. The St. Johns is wide at this point and can be rough on windy days, so stick to the left bank. There is considerable powerboat traffic on the St. Johns, so use caution.

TAKE-OUT (D): The St. Johns passes under SR 46 approximately halfway between Sanford and the coastal city of Mims. The bridge is slightly less than one mile east of the CR 426 intersection in Geneva. A small public park and boat ramp are at the northwest bridge approach.

# Reedy Creek

Take a short trip into Reedy Creek and the effect is striking, almost overpowering—this is natural Florida. Nearly everything about Reedy reinforces this image: the tight central channel that snakes through the interior swampland; the pine, oak and cypress woods that create almost impenetrable canopies impervious to both sun and wind; and the dark tea-colored water stained by the tannin produced from rotting pine and cypress leaves.

Mostly, though, there is the wildlife. The quiet, careful paddler is likely to see many white-tailed deer moving through the adjacent marshland. River otters also make their dens along Reedy Creek, and these playful aquatic mammals frequently frolic alone or in groups, gliding gracefully through the water or running remarkably fast along the shore. Possibly the strangest creatures along the creek, though, are the sirens and amphiumas, large (up to three feet) salamanders that lurk in mud flats and thick vegetation to feed on aquatic plants, invertebrates, frogs, small snakes, or fish. There are also numerous species of birds. Wood ducks, white ibis, ospreys, red-tailed and red-shouldered hawks, wood storks, and black vultures are just a few of the birds that can be seen and heard along the creek.

From the Walt Disney World property, Reedy winds through about 20 miles of swampland, emptying into Lake Russell. It exits from the opposite side of the lake and, five miles downstream, splits into two branches. The Dead River branch runs into Lake Hatchineha, and the Reedy Creek branch empties into Cypress Lake. Along the way, the creek passes beneath several bridges and through one water-control structure. As it traverses the more characteristic swampland, it narrows and branches into many fingers, each shallow and congested with fallen trees and deceiving cypress knees. Even at reasonable water levels, the hardiest of paddlers might find these areas to be impassable. Because of this, the portion of Reedy Creek included in this guide consists of an eight-mile section just south of I-4 west of Orlando. This section is bisected by US 17-92, a main highway between Kissimmee and Lakeland, and the overpass bridge in Intercession City makes a convenient access point for two short out-and-back day-trips.

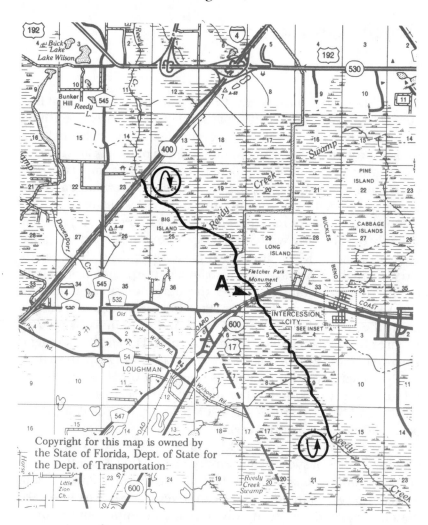

## US 17-92 Bridge (A) in Intercession City to I-4 and Return: 8 miles

DIFFICULTY: Moderate to strenuous
SCENERY: Excellent
COUNTY: Osceola
TOPO QUAD: Intercession City

ACCESS: From Orlando, travel south on I-4 and exit west on US 192. Proceed for two miles, passing the entrance highway to Walt

Disney World. Turn left (south) on CR 545 and travel five miles to the intersection with CR 532. This point can also be reached from locations west of Orlando by leaving eastbound I-4 at the CR 532 exit and proceeding east on that road for 1.25 miles. Three miles east of this point, CR 532 dead-ends at US 17-92. The bridge over Reedy Creek is the third the paddler will encounter after proceeding left (northeast) for one-half mile from CR 532. At this point, there is ample parking and easy access to the creek along a graded path on the northeast side of the bridge.

TRIP DESCRIPTION: From the launching area, turn right and paddle upstream beneath a low railroad bridge and into an area where the pine, oak, and cypress trees form a dense canopy. The first mile of the trip winds through heavy swampland so thick with leaf litter packed among the cypress roots that going ashore is difficult at best. Although there are also numerous side branches, the current makes the main channel easy to follow.

About one mile from the launch area, the creek appears to dead-end in a hyacinth jam just short of a dike; in actuality, it turns sharply to the left into a very narrow canal. This leads outside the forest canopy to a small pond situated at the foot of a water-control structure. A wooden dock on the right is useful for pulling canoes out of the water to portage around the dam. This structure is surrounded by a high fence marked as private property of Walt Disney World, so do not tamper with it. The waterway north of the structure is about 35 feet wide and is not part of the original creek bed, but rather an area dredged out for building a nearby dike. Less than one-quarter mile past the portage, the paddler will bear to the left and re-enter the main channel of Reedy Creek. Bearing sharply to the right, instead, will lead to the dike encountered at the hyacinth jam on the south side of the dam. It also intersects a canal that is easily paddled, which might make an interesting side trip.

For the next two miles, the creek again winds through heavily canopied forest. In several places, there are downed trees necessitating carry-overs, and in one area a series of closely packed cypress trees and knees growing in the water must be carefully negotiated. In general, though, the paddling is not strenuous. Beyond this point, however, the creek narrows and becomes shallow. The current increases, and from three to four miles the going is quite difficult. In this general area the creek passes through a clearing at a power line right-of-way. Just after this, but prior to flowing beneath I-4, the creek becomes highly congested with cypresses and downed trees. This area is so obstructed that the paddler is advised to turn back at this point. Because of the obstructions and the current, the first mile of the return trip requires very careful maneuvering. (Note: though Reedy Creek flows beneath I-4, there is no access from that road.)

## South of US 17-92 Bridge (A) in Intercession City and Return: 8 miles

DIFFICULTY: Moderate to strenuous
SCENERY: Excellent
COUNTY: Osceola
TOPO QUADS: Intercession City, Davenport, Lake Tohopekaliga

ACCESS: (See pages 96–97)

TRIP DESCRIPTION: From the launching area, turn left and paddle beneath the US 17-92 bridge. Just beyond the bridge, the creek narrows and flows past three wooden posts, planted midstream, and then widens again to about 15 or 20 feet. The first two miles of this section provide some very nice paddling as the stream meanders through a cypress swamp with gorgeous scenery. In a few places, though, the water weeds are so tightly packed that a canoe must be pushed through forcibly, and some obstructing overhangs must be negotiated. There are also many branches leading off the central channel, but these are not easily mistaken for the main creek bed.

Between two and three miles, the creek narrows considerably and becomes more congested. Some carry-overs and careful maneuvering are required to negotiate the numerous obstructions encountered. After three miles, the paddling becomes quite strenuous. Fallen trees require many carry-overs and tricky maneuvers. In addition, even the most careful paddler will find it difficult to steer the canoe through the maze of cypress knees. At about four miles, the creek becomes so congested that the canoeist is advised to turn back. The typical paddler should be able to reach the two-mile point in about one hour; however, because of the increased difficulty, the next two miles will take twice that time.

# Arbuckle Creek

Located near Sebring in south central Florida, Arbuckle Creek flows for 23 miles from Lake Arbuckle to Lake Istokpoga, stretching through cypress strands, open grass prairies, ranch land and an occasional oak hammock. Originally, the creek was known to the Indians as *Weokufka,* or "muddy water," although later it was apparently named Arbuckle after a family of local settlers. Lake Istokpoga (Indian for "dangerous waters"), at 27,692 acres, is one of the five largest lakes in the state, and in early spring it is drawn down, causing low-water levels in Arbuckle Creek.

For the first ten miles, the creek runs along the western border of Avon Park Bombing Range. A portion of this range is a wildlife management area and becomes very active with hunters during the winter hunting season. Fishing is very productive in the creek with fine concentrations of bass, bluegill and shellcracker; wild turkey are frequently seen along the banks. The paddler will likely encounter some boaters and fishermen along the waterway and, in general, will find them quite friendly.

This guide covers the creek from Lake Arbuckle to US 98, three miles upstream of Lake Istokpoga. Access is provided at four convenient boat ramps, although the shuttle route between several of them is long and awkward. The middle section of the stream, between Arbuckle Road and Arbuckle Creek Road, is prone to severe hyacinth jams near the end, so the paddler is cautioned to question local boaters or fish camps concerning the status of this section.

### Lake Arbuckle to Arbuckle Road (A–B): 2.3 miles

DIFFICULTY: Moderate
SCENERY: Excellent
COUNTIES: Polk, Highlands
TOPO QUADS: Lake Arbuckle, Lake Arbuckle NE

ACCESS: The put-in at Lake Arbuckle is at a boat ramp located in a fish camp just outside the main gate of the Avon Park Bombing Range. It is reached from the town of Avon Park by traveling 10.5

miles east of US 27-98 on SR 64. The fish camp is on the left (north) side of the road just west of the bridge over Arbuckle Creek. Access is down a concrete ramp (there is a small launching fee).

TRIP DESCRIPTION: This is unquestionably the most scenic section along the entire creek. It snakes through a dense cypress swamp and is lined with tall trees shading a large percentage of the waterway. The channel is only about 30 feet wide and the current is swift, as indicated by the bottom vegetation bending to follow the flow. Numerous overhangs, deadfalls and submerged logs

*Isolated beaches are scattered along Arbuckle Creek.*

obstruct the creek, requiring careful maneuvering to negotiate. Some of the overhangs contain large hornet nests which, for obvious reasons, should be avoided. Wildlife is abundant and it is not uncommon to see turtles, barred owls and red-tailed hawks.

The boat ramp is on the south shore of Lake Arbuckle. After launching, the paddler should circle to the right around a large area of aquatic grasses. A large fishing dock, belonging to the Avon Park Air Force Base, will appear on the left (east) and then a very narrow passage through the grasses will lead to the SR 64 bridge and the entrance to the creek.

The pilings from an old railroad trestle will be encountered 2.1 miles from the put-in. After 0.2 mile, the paddler will pass a house on the west shore, then turn sharply to the right into a short dredged canal that leads to the take-out on Arbuckle Road.

## Arbuckle Road to Arbuckle Creek Road (B–C): 9.3 miles

DIFFICULTY: Easy
SCENERY: Good
COUNTY: Highlands
TOPO QUADS: Lake Arbuckle NE, Lake Arbuckle SE

ACCESS: The boat ramp on Arbuckle Road is reached from the town of Avon Park by traveling eight miles east of US 27 on SR 64. Turn right (east) onto Arbuckle Road, which is graded, and continue for three miles until the road dead-ends near a house. The boat ramp is located just west of this house, with ample parking nearby.

TRIP DESCRIPTION: Before attempting this section of the creek, the paddler would do well to check with local boaters or fish camps concerning any obstructions to through-traffic. A wide lakelike area in the creek, about one mile upstream of the take-out at Arbuckle Creek Road, is prone to severe hyacinth jams and could force the traveler into a long, difficult portage through a cypress swamp on the east or along a heavily overgrown dike on the west.

From the boat ramp, proceed down a short canal and turn right onto the creek. After 0.3 mile, the right (west) shoreline opens up into ranch land while a dense cypress swamp remains on the other shore. About 1.4 miles later, the creek narrows and the

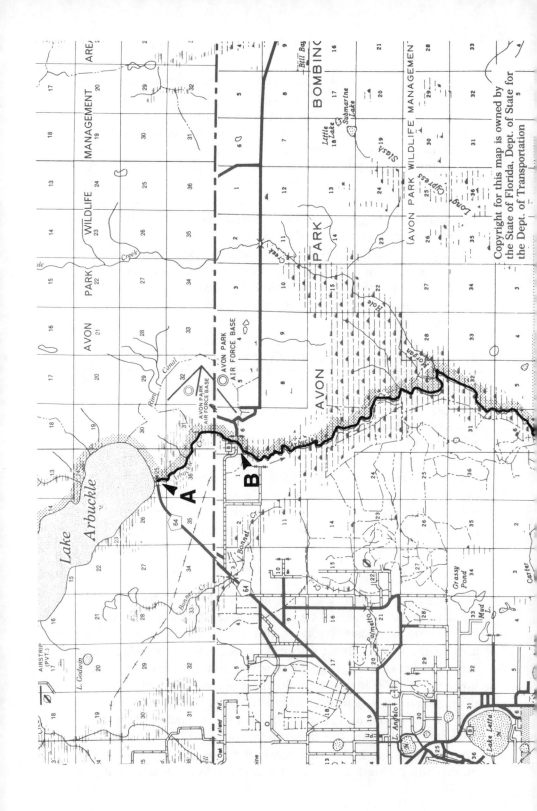

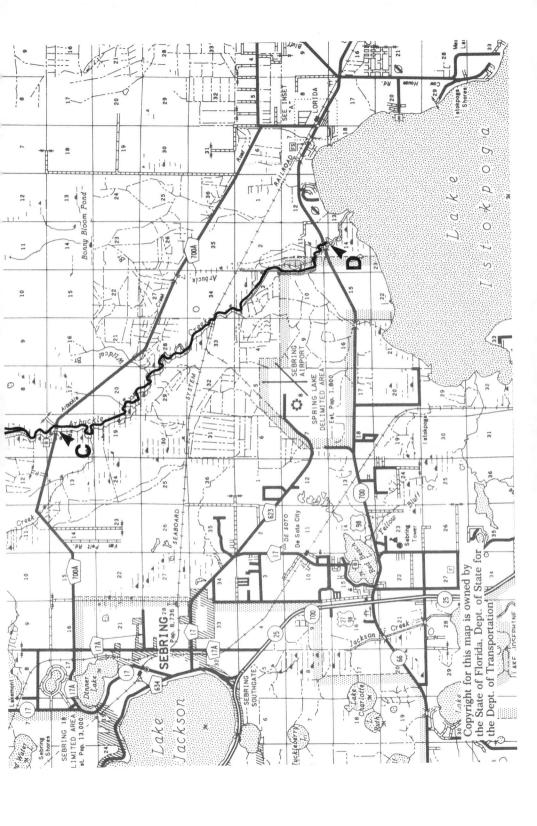

swamp emerges again on the western bank. This terrain continues until about four miles into the trip, at which point Morgan Hole Creek enters on the left side, and the surrounding vegetation opens up. Marsh grass on the east and a high dike on the west line the creek.

Eight miles from the put-in, the creek separates into two channels. The one to the right follows the dike past a rancher's culvert and pumping station, while the left passage flows through a cypress stand. Both lead into the wide, lakelike area described earlier. The Arbuckle Creek Road bridge is about a mile downstream of this point. The take-out is at a ramp on the right (west) immediately upstream of the bridge.

## Arbuckle Creek Road to US 98 (C–D): 8.8 miles

DIFFICULTY: Easy to moderate (one short whitewater shoal)
SCENERY: Good
COUNTY: Highlands
TOPO QUADS: Lake Arbuckle SE, Lorida

ACCESS: From SR 64 in Avon Park, proceed south on SR 17 and continue to follow it as it zigzags for 6.8 miles past Lakes Lotela and Letta to the intersection with CR 17-A, or Arbuckle Creek Road. Turn left (east) and drive for 6.1 miles to the bridge over Arbuckle Creek. The boat ramp is on the northwest bridge approach.

TRIP DESCRIPTION: For the first 4.5 miles of this section, the creek traverses open ranch land. Although there are numerous pockets of cypress, oak, and some Florida holly, they are too widely scattered to provide shade. The next 1.5 miles pass through a dense oak forest with an abundance of small areas for good campsites, including an excellent spot 100 yards north of the railroad bridge 5.5 miles from the put-in. The site is on the east shoreline and overlooks a small rapid formed by a series of limestone rocks and a drop in the creek bed. The rapids should be run over two small standing waves just to the left of an islet on the right side of the channel. At low water, exposed rocks in midcreek and a limestone ledge along the left make it very difficult to negotiate this area.

*Arbuckle Creek*

One-half mile past the rapids, the main creek channel enters a man-made canal. Tall spoil banks are partially vegetated and interrupted only by cuts where the original creek bed, now overgrown with aquatic plants, meanders across the canal. About one mile from the take-out, the canal begins to follow the original channel as it snakes gently past a cypress swamp on the left. Immediately after the creek passes under the US 98 bridge, the paddler will encounter a fish camp on the right. The take-out is up a concrete boat ramp into the camp, where there will be a nominal ramp-users' charge.

TAKE-OUT (D): The take-out is reached from the boat ramp at Arbuckle Creek Road by traveling east on that road for nine miles until it forms a "T" with a crossing road. To the left (north) is a graded lane, and to the right is the continuation of Arbuckle Creek Road. Turn right and proceed for 1.2 miles to US 98 in the town of Lorida. Turn right (west) and travel for three miles to the bridge over Arbuckle Creek. Neibert Fishing Resort is located on the southwest approach to the bridge.

# Peace River

The Green Swamp, northeast of Tampa, is the headwaters for four of the finest rivers in the state: the Oklawaha, Withlacoochee, Hillsborough, and Peace. The Peace River flows for approximately 133 miles from Lake Hancock near Bartow in Polk County to Charlotte Harbor near Punta Gorda. The river basin encompasses 2,400 square miles of primarily agricultural and ranch land, and along the river's entire length, numerous creeks and streams empty their contents into it. The Peace is considered to be one of the 13 major coastal rivers in Florida, which means it has an average discharge at its mouth of 1,000 cfs or more. As might be expected, almost 70 percent on the average of the annual flow in the river occurs from June through October, after the onset of the wet summer weather. Despite the high nutrient levels caused by the discharge from phosphate mines and agriculture, the river retains a fair water quality and indeed supports a fine population of fish.

The Peace River is steeped in a rich natural and cultural history. In 1842, by virtue of an agreement between General Worth and the infamous Indian chief, Billy Bowlegs, the Peace was established as the boundary between Indian territory to the east and land for the white man to the west. During the Seminole Wars, numerous battles occurred along the banks of the Peace. At the confluence of the Peace and Payne Creek, south of Bowling Green, the Seminole Indians attacked a trading post at the start of the Third Seminole War, and one of the last battles of that war was fought near Fort Meade.

The Peace River can be paddled for almost 90 miles from Fort Meade to near Fort Ogden. This guide only covers the middle Peace from Zolfo Springs to Gardner, the section of the river considered by many to have the finest scenery and best camping opportunities. Narrow deep channels with high banks alternate with broad sections and quiet pools as the river passes through dense woodlands. Sand bluffs give way to shoreline flats, thickly carpeted with grasses and enclosed by the surrounding woods, making ideal campsites. The nearby forest abounds with deer and other wildlife, and the observant paddler will see numerous bird species, including herons, egrets, and kingfishers.

106

## Zolfo Springs to Gardner Boat Ramp (A–B): 20 miles

DIFFICULTY: Easy
SCENERY: Excellent
COUNTY: Hardee
TOPO QUADS: Zolfo Springs, Gardner

ACCESS: The small town of Zolfo Springs is located about 45 miles east of Bradenton on SR 64 and 18 miles west of Avon Park on that same road. It can also be reached from Lakeland by traveling south on US 98 to Fort Meade and then continuing south on US 17 for 17 miles. The put-in is at a small county park called Pioneer Park on the northwest corner of the SR 64–US 17 intersection. This park has a fine concrete ramp for boat launching, numerous developed campsites placed amid the trees, and clean restroom facilities.

TRIP DESCRIPTION: Although this section can be paddled in a single day, that would do it an injustice—it is ideal for camping. Despite the large number of groups using this river on busy weekends, fine campsites are so numerous that you can be virtually certain of finding one. A word of warning, though, for all paddlers: the majority of land along this section is private property, owned by the Ben Hill Griffin Peace River Ranch; and they have a decided policy against campers using the eastern shore of the river. This policy will be made strikingly clear by the countless "No Trespassing" signs stationed along the left bank. The western shore, except for a few posted areas, is open for camping.

The launch area at Pioneer Park is down a concrete ramp into a small pond connected to the river by a short canal. From the canal, turn left (west) and proceed downstream. At low water, a V-formation of rocks here will create a small shoal. Half a mile from the put-in, the river will pass beneath the SR 64 bridge, the last such structure you'll encounter until an old wooden bridge at 13 miles.

Tall bluffs on the left support a forest of palms, oaks, and cypress draped with Spanish moss and broadleaf kudzu vines.

In the cool, dry winter season—also the prime time for canoe camping—the river will run nominally low. This will expose numerous sandbars and create shallow pools. In addition, deadfalls and normally submerged logs will surface. Although

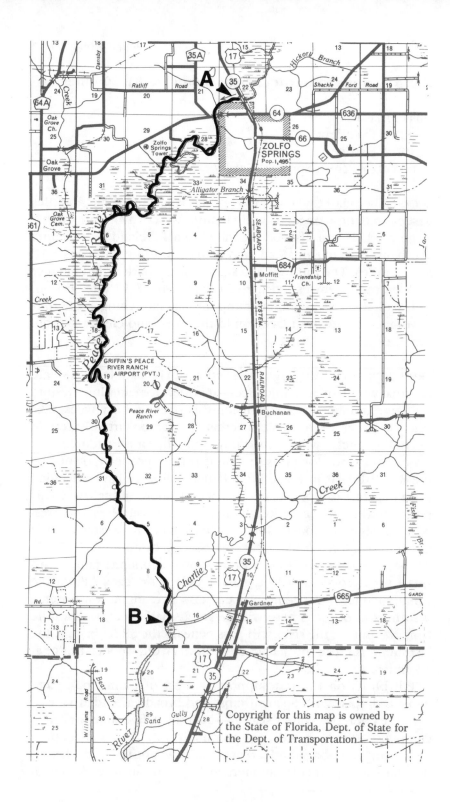

*The Peace River sweeps canoeists through a gap in an old dam in Zolfo Springs.*

minor obstacles for the canoeist and kayaker, these features prove to be major obstructions for powerboaters and may restrict their access to this section of the Peace, a blessing for all paddlers.

Several side streams intersect the river along this section. Troublesome, Hickory, Oak, and Limestone creeks enter from the west, and Charlie Creek, the largest contributor, comes in from the east. Charlie Creek is also called Charlie Apopka Creek, a corruption of an Indian name which translates literally as "trout (*Tsala,* or Charlie) eating place" (*Apopka*). Limestone Creek is a very descriptive name. It flows into the Peace about 16.5 miles from the put-in, and its presence is announced far in advance by the appearance of limestone rock formations along the banks. The banks of Limestone Creek are also lined with rock and, at low water, the undercutting due to erosion is clearly visible.

The take-out at the Gardner boat ramp is three miles downstream of Limestone Creek. It is located on the left (east) side of the river and identified in advance by a small sign hanging over the river.

TAKE-OUT (B): The boat ramp is reached from Zolfo Springs by traveling south on US 17 for 10.2 miles past SR 64 to the town of Gardner. Turn right (west) onto a graded road identified by a small sign for a public boat ramp. Continue on this road for 1.5 miles until it dead-ends at the boat ramp. There is ample parking in the area.

# Part IV:
# Waterways of
# the Everglades

# Blackwater River

The Blackwater River is part of a 13.5-mile canoe circuit that winds through Collier-Seminole State Park wilderness preserve. This preserve is at the western extreme of the Everglades and features a prime example of the mangrove forest that forms the outer rim of south Florida. The canoe circuit includes tidal creeks and bays as well as the Blackwater River. A diverse community of wildlife, including roseate spoonbills and manatees, inhabits the preserve. The tides add another dimension to paddling in the preserve. Current in the creeks becomes moderately swift during tidal change, and even the Blackwater River reverses flow on the incoming tide.

## Collier-Seminole State Park Loop (A): 13.5 miles

DIFFICULTY: Moderate
SCENERY: Outstanding
COUNTY: Collier
TOPO QUAD: Royal Palm Hammock
NAUTICAL CHART: Lostmans River to Wiggins Pass (11430)

ACCESS: Collier-Seminole State Park is 15 miles southeast of the Gulf Coast town of Naples on US 41. The park is also 75 miles west of Miami on the section of US 41 known as the Tamiami Trail—the famous road through the Everglades. The park charges admission and ramp fees. Only a limited number of canoes is permitted in the preserve each day, so an advance phone call to the park is recommended. The park telephone is (941) 394-3397.

TRIP DESCRIPTION: There are special requirements for canoeing at Collier-Seminole. All paddlers must file a float plan at the entrance station. This requirement is dictated by the high potential for getting lost among the myriad of mangrove islands. The rangers will brief all paddlers on the tide situation and stress the necessity for compass and map (the nautical chart is recommended). All paddlers doing the entire loop must travel

112

counterclockwise through Mud Bay to Palm Bay and then up the Blackwater River. Finally, those attempting the complete circuit in a day are required to be on the water by 9 A.M.

The trip commences at the Collier-Seminole boat ramp. The first one-half mile is on a wide man-made channel to the Blackwater River. The upper river is narrow and winds through a mangrove forest. The red mangrove with its characteristic prop roots forms the first echelon of mangrove. The black mangrove, with its hundreds of pencil-like pneumatophore roots sticking out of the muck, is back on higher ground. The trail leaves the Blackwater River at 1.8 miles, where a sign directs paddlers to turn right into a tidal creek. This narrow creek almost forms a tunnel through the mangrove. A small bay marks the two-mile point, and Mud Bay is close at hand.

Those arriving at Mud Bay at low tide will soon discover the source of the name, as there are areas where canoes must be pulled over mud bars. Bear to the left toward the large island upon entering the bay. Keep to the left side of the island and head

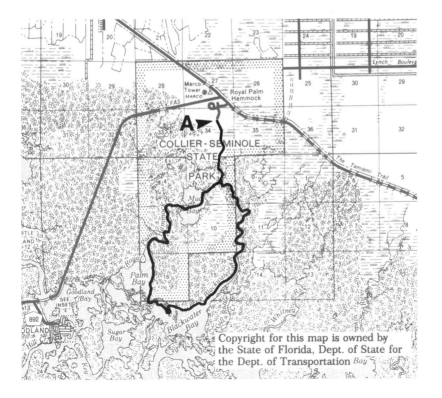

into Royal Palm Hammock Creek. West Palm Run comes in on the right as Royal Palm Hammock Creek turns to the south. The Old Grove, one of only two spots of high ground on this trip, is passed on the left at 3.5 miles.

Grocery Place, the other high point and designated camping area, is on the right at 4.5 miles at the mouth of a stream. Early settlers arranged for supply boats to cache provisions on this spot, thus the origin of the name. Royal Palm Hammock Creek enters the open expanse of Palm Bay downstream of Grocery Place. Paddlers should stick to the left bank from this point until reentering Blackwater River.

The paddler enters the Ten Thousand Islands region at six miles, and it is very easy to get lost here among the numerous look-alike mangrove islands. For this reason it is essential to keep the mainland to the immediate left of the canoe. Another mile of paddling and Blackwater Bay is entered. Continue bearing left and go into the mouth of the Blackwater River. Channel markers are spaced at intervals going up the river. A branch of Gill Rattle Creek is passed on the right at 7.5 miles, as is another side stream at 10.0 miles.

*Mud Bay*

# Everglades City and Ten Thousand Islands

Everglades City is the hub of paddling activity in the western Everglades. It is located on the northern shore of Chokoloskee Bay and provides direct access to the well-known Ten Thousand Islands area, which has been classified by the state as an Aquatic Preserve. This myriad of islands forms countless passes and small bays. The fishing is excellent and the islands present an incredible number of fine camping opportunities.

The Ten Thousand Islands face directly onto the Gulf of Mexico, which makes them subject to the whims of weather systems coming ashore off the open water. The paddler is cautioned to check on weather conditions before venturing into the area and, once there, should always be prepared, of course, for sudden changes in wind or weather conditions.

Because of the almost infinite number of paddling opportunities in Ten Thousand Islands, this guide will not attempt to cover any of the trails in this area. Instead, the interested paddler should consult the personnel at the Everglades National Park Ranger Station in Everglades City. These people know the area and can provide valuable information concerning interesting paddling trails for both day and overnight use. The ranger station is located on Chokoloskee Bay in south Everglades City, on the west side of CR 29, just north of where that road becomes a causeway.

# Wilderness Waterway

Extending for nearly 100 miles, from Everglades City in the northwest Everglades to Flamingo in the southern reaches of the National Park land mass, the Wilderness Waterway crosses some of the most unique terrain in the country. It winds through rivers, creeks, and large bays as it traverses mangrove wilderness and sawgrass prairies. This predominantly estuarine area is home to countless marine species, including dolphins and manatees, as well as a large variety of beautiful wading birds such as roseate spoonbills and ibis. Of course, any paddler who ventures into the Glades is likely to see one of its main attractions, the alligator.

The minimum time required for a canoe trip across the Wilderness Waterway is one week. It can be done faster, but seven days provide sufficient buffer for delays due to weather and unplanned sight-seeing excursions. The National Park Service has constructed a series of campsites and camping platforms (called chickees) along, as well as in the general vicinity of, the Waterway. These can be used by paddlers traversing the entire waterway or taking shorter trips. The Park Service requires all back-country campers to obtain camping permits and file float plans. This can be done at the Everglades City Ranger Station or the ranger's office at the Flamingo Visitor Center. Plans are required for safety and to ensure that campsites don't become overburdened.

Detailed coverage of the Wilderness Waterway is beyond the scope of this guide. For more information, the interested paddler should contact personnel at either the Flamingo or Everglades City ranger stations. In addition, a copy of *A Guide to the Wilderness Waterway of the Everglades National Park* by William G. Truesdale is well worth the money. It contains a series of maps, which lead the paddler across the waterway, as well as a narrative covering the natural and cultural history of the area. Finally, a set of nautical charts for the Everglades National Park is highly recommended for both on-water navigation as well as pre-trip planning. These include chart number 11433 (Everglades National Park Whitewater Bay), chart 11432 (Shark River to Lostmans River), and chart 11430 (Lostmans River to Wiggins Pass). Nautical charts are available at most marinas as well as the National Park ranger stations and visitor centers.

# Turner River

Many paddlers consider the Turner River one of the finest canoe trails in the Everglades. Flowing into Chokoloskee Bay, it meanders from the northeast for about ten miles, passing through several types of mangrove forests, a large marshland of sawgrass, and several areas of high ground richly vegetated with tall pines and old oaks. Numerous side streams intersect the Turner, inviting exploration. Some end in impassable overgrowth, while others lead to interesting little bays. The river flows from north to south into Chokoloskee Bay, although within a few miles of the mouth of the river, the tides affect the direction of current.

The river was named after Richard B. Turner, a Seminole War scout who guided a military expedition up "Chokolisca Creek" in 1857. This trip resulted in several armed conflicts that effectively ended the Third Seminole War. In the early 1870s, Turner moved onto the river and built a homestead; its remains can still be seen along the eastern shore.

This guide covers the river from Chokoloskee Island to the Tamiami Trail; however, due to the nature of the river, it can easily be paddled in either direction.

## Chokoloskee Island to Tamiami Trail (A–B): 9.3 miles

DIFFICULTY: Easy to moderate (some areas of confusing multiple channels)
SCENERY: Excellent
COUNTY: Collier
TOPO QUADS: Chokoloskee, Ochopee

ACCESS: Everglades City is located about three miles south of US 41, or Tamiami Trail, on CR 29. To reach Chokoloskee Island, drive 2.5 miles south of Everglades City on the CR 29 causeway. A large opening in the roadside vegetation on the left (east) side of the road about 100 yards north of the island marks the put-in point. There is ample and safe parking along the road in this area.

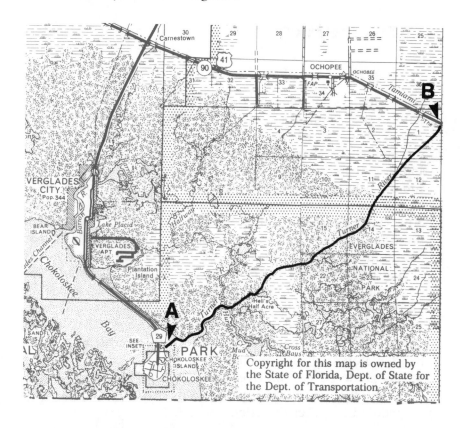

Copyright for this map is owned by
the State of Florida, Dept. of State for
the Dept. of Transportation.

TRIP DESCRIPTION: From the put-in, the mouth of the Turner River can be seen almost due east across Chokoloskee Bay. Care should be taken when crossing the bay, especially when windy conditions kick up a mild chop. Additionally, near the mouth of the river, there are a number of oyster beds to be avoided, as well as mud flats which appear during low tide.

One and one-half miles into the trip, a large shell mound on the right (east) marks the location of the old Turner homestead. The Left Hand Turner River comes in from the north one-half mile later, and a short distance beyond that, Hurddles Creek enters from the south. From this point on, the Turner narrows gradually and begins to snake its way northeast.

For the next several miles, it's a very good idea to navigate with a topo map and compass, as this will help distinguish the myriad of side streams from the main channel. From five to seven miles, the river passes through a series of small lakes and open areas connected by short creeks and an occasional mangrove tunnel.

At 7.5 miles, the main river turns toward the north, while the paddler should continue in a northeasterly direction along the Turner River Canal. The banks of the canal, which was dug many years ago, are overgrown with lush vegetation teeming with wildlife. One and one-half miles into this scenic passage, the paddler will encounter the Tamiami Trail bridge. There are two take-outs: one on the southwest side of the bridge and one on the northwest side at H. P. Williams Park.

TAKE-OUT (B): H. P. Williams Park can be reached from Everglades City by proceeding north on CR 29 to the intersection with US 41, or Tamiami Trail. Turn right (east) and proceed for 6.5 miles to the bridge over the Turner River Canal. The wayside park, located on the northwest bridge approach, has a large parking area and picnic facilities.

# Everglades National Park

Everglades National Park encompasses 1.4 million acres of prime Everglades and constitutes the entire tip of peninsular Florida. The Everglades is a water world of shallow bays and lakes, flooded prairies, and narrow creeks. The early Calusa Indians recognized the canoe as the best mode of transportation through the Everglades, and today the canoe is still the best way to appreciate its beauty and wonder. The Park Service has established a system of marked canoe trails within the park. The focal point of paddle sport and other park activities is at Flamingo, down at Cape Sable.

Flamingo is at the end of a 50-mile drive from Florida City that passes through mangrove forests, cypress stands, coastal and marl prairies, sloughs and hammocks. Observation and interpretive facilities are located along the road. Before attempting any of the canoe trails, paddlers should stop at the Flamingo Visitor Center for trail maps and current information on trail conditions and the

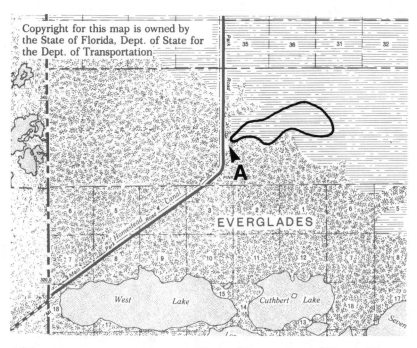

bug situation. Low water can be a problem during the dry winter season and bugs, especially mosquitoes, can be unbearable during the warm months. Because of the flat terrain and lack of distinctive landmarks, map and compass are basic equipment for Everglades canoeing.

This book describes two of Everglades National Park's day-use canoe trails. Nine Mile Pond loop offers a taste of the awe-inspiring openness of an Everglades freshwater marl prairie. Mud Lake loop trail is known for good birding and passes through mangrove-lined lakes, streams, and canals.

## Nine Mile Pond Loop Trail (A): 5.2 miles

DIFFICULTY: Easy (strenuous at low water)
SCENERY: Outstanding
COUNTY: Dade
TOPO QUAD: Mahogany Hammock

ACCESS: Nine Mile Pond is 27 miles from the Main Visitor Center on the road to Flamingo and 12 miles from the Flamingo Visitor Center. Look for the Nine Mile Pond canoe trail sign.

TRIP DESCRIPTION: The trip begins with a paddle across Nine Mile Pond out through a narrow, mangrove-shrouded channel. The trail is indicated by white pole markers. Tree islands with coco-plum and buttonwood dot the surroundings. A near-surface limestone layer limits the size of red mangroves that grow in small clusters.

The trail soon enters an open area of spike rush. The open expanse and sheer quietness of the landscape are impressive. No motors are allowed here, and the only sounds are the wind through the rushes augmented by insects and birds. Below the waterline, the rushes are coated with an alga that gives rise to the term "breadstick." Paddling through the rushes is strenuous at low water. While out on the trail, check the sky for bald eagles. These raptors, rare in many parts of the country, are seen frequently in the Everglades.

Finally, the trail passes through two small ponds and then reenters Nine Mile Pond. Take the opportunity to do some birding while passing through these ponds.

*Freshwater marl prairie, Nine Mile Pond*

## Mud Lake Loop Trail (B): 4.8 miles

DIFFICULTY: Easy
SCENERY: Excellent
COUNTY: Monroe
TOPO QUAD: Flamingo
NAUTICAL CHART: Everglades National Park (11433)

ACCESS: The put-in is on Bear Lake Road 2.2 miles from Flamingo Visitor Center. Bear Lake Road parallels the west bank of Buttonwood Canal and intersects the main park road about half a mile northeast of The Flamingo Visitor Center. The turnoff is well-marked with a sign.

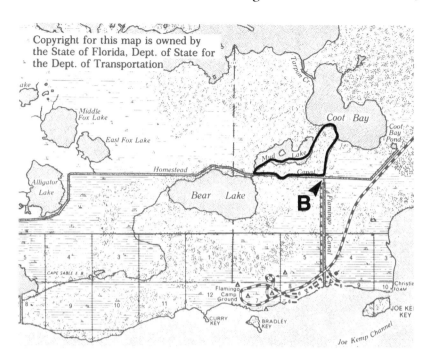

TRIP DESCRIPTION: The canoe trail is laid out in a clockwise direction with numbered posts. The first 1.6 miles lie along the mangrove-shrouded channel of the old Homestead Canal. This canal is a remnant of an earlier time when canals were dug in an effort to exploit the Everglades. About a mile up the canal, the canal dodges around Bear Lake Mound—a Calusa Indian relic.

A channel to the right leads into the shallow waters of Mud Lake. This is a good birding lake, and roseate spoonbills frequent the area. The trail takes a northeast tack across Mud Lake past a peninsula on the north shore and into Mud Lake Creek. This creek is believed to be one of many canals that Calusa Indians constructed to facilitate canoe travel through the Everglades.

The short trip through Mud Lake Creek leads into Coot Bay. In pre-park days there was an active charcoal-making industry along its shore. Buttonwood trees were cut down, stacked, and burned to make charcoal for sale to settlers in the area. Turn to the right after entering Coot Bay and paddle along the south shore. The natural tranquility is compromised by powerboats that share Coot Bay.

A little over one mile of paddling leads to the entrance of Buttonwood Canal, which once led directly to Florida Bay; the effects of saltwater intrusion proved very damaging to plant and animal communities, so the canal was plugged. The take-out dock is 0.8 mile down the canal, on the right.

# East Everglades

Manatee Bay lies at the eastern extreme of the Everglades where US 1 starts its over-water trip through the Florida Keys. This mangrove-and-marsh country is punctuated with streams and small lakes ideal for canoe exploration. A large variety of marine birdlife calls this area home, and the endangered manatee is occasionally seen. Two of the possible paddle trips are described here.

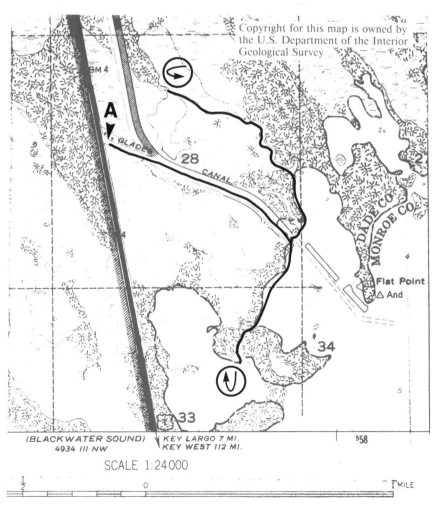

A

BM 4

GLADE

28

CANAL

DADE CO

MONROE CO

Flat Point

△ And

4

34

5

(BLACKWATER SOUND)    KEY LARGO 7 MI.
   4934 III NW            KEY WEST 112 MI.

558

SCALE 1:24000

½        0                                        1 MILE

125

## US 1 (A) to Morris Lake and Return: 4 miles

DIFFICULTY: Easy
SCENERY: Good
COUNTY: Dade
TOPO QUAD: Glades

ACCESS: The closest put-in is at a private marina on the east side of US 1, 12 miles south of the intersection of the Turnpike Extension and US 1 in Florida City. A small launching fee is charged.

TRIP DESCRIPTION: The trip begins with a one-mile paddle down the Aerojet Canal. Turn left and head north upon entering Manatee Bay. Paddle 0.3 mile along the shoreline. Morris Creek is the second stream encountered. It splits into two streams 0.4 mile upstream from its mouth. Take the left-hand stream for the remaining 0.3 mile into Morris Lake.

## US 1 (A) to Sarge Lake and Return: 3.2 miles

DIFFICULTY: Easy
SCENERY: Good
COUNTY: Dade
TOPO QUAD: Glades

ACCESS: See Morris Lake above.

TRIP DESCRIPTION: The first mile of the trip is down the Aerojet Canal. After entering Manatee Bay, turn right and follow the shoreline 0.4 mile south to Sarge Creek. This creek connects Sarge Lake to Manatee Bay and is only 0.2 mile long.

# Glossary

**Baseflow**   That part of a stream flow that comes from springs or groundwater seepage.

**DOT**   Department of Transportation.

**Deadfall**   A tree or tree limb that has fallen across a stream.

**Drainage**   An area from which surface runoff is carried by a stream and its tributaries (same as watershed).

**Estuary**   Where fresh and saltwater mix and ocean tides assume control of local water dynamics.

**Hammock**   A long-standing community consisting mainly of hardwood trees and with very little undergrowth.

**Headwaters**   The source of a stream.

**Hydrilla**   A non-native aquatic plant that frequently obstructs passage through a waterway.

**Lagoon**   A body of water separated from the sea by a barrier island.

**Meander**   A loop in a river's course through an adjacent floodplain.

**Midden**   A shell mound.

**Oxbow**   A crescent-shaped lake formed when a stream cuts through the ends of a former meander.

**Portage**   To carry a boat and gear around an obstacle in a stream or between two bodies of water.

**Potable water**   Water that can be consumed safely by humans.

**Rapids**   An area of turbulence caused by swift water moving over obstructions in the streambed.

**Shuttle**   The movement of several vehicles, such that one is left at the put-in and another is left at the take-out.

**Slough**   A stagnant swamp or marsh with an imperceptible flow that increases at high-water levels.

**Snag**   A submerged object that can catch a paddle or boat hull.

**Switchback**   Where a stream doubles back on itself.

**USGS**   United States Geological Survey.

# Canoe Liveries and Outfitters

## Alafia River

Alafia Canoe Rentals
4419 River Drive
Valrico, FL 33594
(813) 689-8645

## Blackwater River

Collier-Seminole State Park
20200 E. Tamiami Trail
Naples, FL 34114
(941) 394-3397

## Bulow Creek

Bulow Plantation Ruins State
Park
Historical Site
P.O. Box 655
Bunnell, FL 32110
(904) 517-2084

## Ding Darling National Wildlife Refuge

Captiva Kayak Company
P.O. Box 122
Captiva Island, FL 33924
(941) 395-2925

'Tween Waters Marina
15951 Captiva Road
Captiva Island, FL 33924
(941) 472-5161

## Econlockhatchee River

Hidden River RV Park
15295 E. Colonial Drive
Orlando, FL 32826
(407) 568-5346
www.hiddenriverrvpark.com

## Estero River

Estero River Outfitters
20991 S. Tamiami Trail
Estero, FL 33928
(941) 992-4050
www.all-florida.com/
saestero.htm

## Everglades Region

Florida Bay Outfitters
P.O. Box 2513
Key Largo, FL 33037
(305) 451-3018

Flamingo Lodge Marina and
Outpost Resort
No. 1 Flamingo Lodge
Highway
Flamingo, FL 33034
(941) 695-3101

Glades Haven RV Park and
Marina
South State Road 29
P.O. Box 443

Everglades City, FL 33929
(941) 695-2746
www.gladeshaven.com

North American Canoe Tours
Everglades Outpost and Ivy
House
P.O. Box 5038
Everglades City, FL 33929
(941) 695-4666

**Hillsborough River**

Hillsborough River State Park
15402 U.S. 301 North
Thonotosassa, FL 33592
(813) 987-6771

Canoe Escape, Inc.
9335 E. Fowler Avenue
Thonotosassa, FL 33592
(813) 986-2067
www.canoeescape.com

**Little Manatee River**

Canoe Outpost–Little
Manatee
18001 U.S. 301 South
Wimauma, FL 33598
(813) 634-2228
www.canoeoutpost.com

**Loxahatchee River**

Canoe Outfitters of Florida
16346 106th Terrace North
Jupiter, FL 33478
(407) 746-7053

Jonathan Dickinson State
Park
16450 S.E. Federal Highway
Hobe Sound, FL 33455
(561) 546-2771

**Manatee River**

KC's River Lodge
1220 Mill Creek Road
Bradenton, FL 34202
(941) 746-6884
www.kcsriverlodge.com

Florida Osprey Boat Tours
P.O. Box 20967
Bradenton, FL 20967
(941) 745-9649

Ray's Canoe Hideaway
1247 Hagle Park Road
Bradenton, FL 34202
(941) 747-3909
www.rayscanoehideaway.com

**Peace River**

Canoe Outpost–Peace River
2816 NW CR 661
Arcadia, FL 34266
(863) 494-1215
www.canoeoutpost.com

Canoe Safari
3020 NW CR 661
Arcadia, FL 34266
(863) 494-7865
www.canoesafari.com

**Tomoka River**

Tomoka State Park
2099 North Beach Street
Ormond Beach, FL 32174
(904) 676-4050

**Miscellaneous**

You may be able to find other
liveries and outfitters from
the following addresses:

Professional Paddlesports
Association—Florida
P.O. Box 1764
Arcadia, FL 34265

Florida Department of
Environmental Protection
Twin Towers Office Building
2600 Blair Stone Road
Tallahassee, FL 32399
(850) 488-1554
www.dep.state.fl.us/parks

# Further Reading

Amos, Stephen H., and William H. Amos. *Atlantic and Gulf Coasts*. New York: Alfred A. Knopf, 1985.

Douglas, Marjory Stoneman. *The Everglades: River of Grass*. St. Simons Island, Ga.: Mockingbird Books, 1947.

Fernald, Edward A., and Donald J. Patton, *Water Resources of Florida*. Tallahassee: Florida State University, 1984.

Grow, Gerald. *Florida Parks: A Guide to Camping in Florida*. Tallahassee: Longleaf Publications, 1981.

Jahoda, Gloria. *River of the Golden Ibis*. New York: Holt, Rinehart & Winston, 1973.

Matthews, Janet Snyder. *Edge of Wilderness: A Settlement History of the Manatee River and Sarasota Bay*. Sarasota: Coastal Press, 1983.

Niering, William A. *Wetlands*. New York: Alfred A. Knopf, 1985.

Teal, John and Mildred. *Life and Death of the Salt Marsh*. New York: Ballantine Books, 1969.

Tebeau, Charlton W. *Man in the Everglades, 2000 Years of Human History in the Everglades National Park*. Coral Gables: University of Miami Press, 1968.

# Index

# About the Authors

*Lou Glaros* was born in Pennsylvania, but grew up in northwest Indiana. After graduating from Purdue University, he moved to Orlando, Florida, where he currently works with a major engineering firm. Active in hiking, camping, wildlife observation, and canoeing, Lou is an avid outdoor enthusiast and belongs to several related organizations, including Peninsula Paddling Club, Florida Sport Paddling Club, Audubon, and Florida Trail Association. Although an experienced canoe tripper, Lou's special interest is freestyle paddling, and he is currently working on an instruction guide to be published soon.

*Doug Sphar* lives on the banks of the St. Johns River in central Florida, where he is active in canoeing, hiking, and camping. He spent his early childhood in Pennsylvania, then moved to Florida as a teenager and learned to paddle and camp along the fringes of the Everglades. Besides his Florida paddling experience, Doug has eight major backpacking trips and canoe tours of U.S. and Canadian boundary waters and Canada's Algonquin Park. He is a member of several outdoor sport groups, including the Florida Sport Paddling Club, Peninsula Paddling Club and Florida Trail Association, where for five years he was Section Leader for FTA trails in the Tosohatchee State Preserve. He works as a systems engineer.